SIDESADDLES AND GEYSERS

Women's Adventures in Old Yellowstone

1874–1903

EDITED BY

M. MARK MILLER

TWODOT®

GUILFORD, CONNECTICUT
HELENA, MONTANA

An imprint of The Rowman & Littlefield Publishing Group, Inc.
4501 Forbes Blvd., Ste. 200
Lanham, MD 20706
www.rowman.com

Distributed by NATIONAL BOOK NETWORK

British Library Cataloguing in Publication Information available

Library of Congress Cataloging-in-Publication Data available

ISBN 978-1-4930-5545-6 (paperback)
ISBN 978-1-4930-5546-3 (electronic)

♾ The paper used in this publication meets the minimum requirements of American National Standard for Information Sciences—Permanence of Paper for Printed Library Materials, ANSI/NISO Z39.48-1992.

This book is dedicated to my fellow volunteer at the Gallatin History Museum in Bozeman, Helen Backlin. She has always been an eager reader of my drafts and an enthusiastic seller of my books, as well as the finest of friends.

Travel in Yellowstone Park could be difficult as these tourists discovered when they had to repair their broken carriage.

Contents

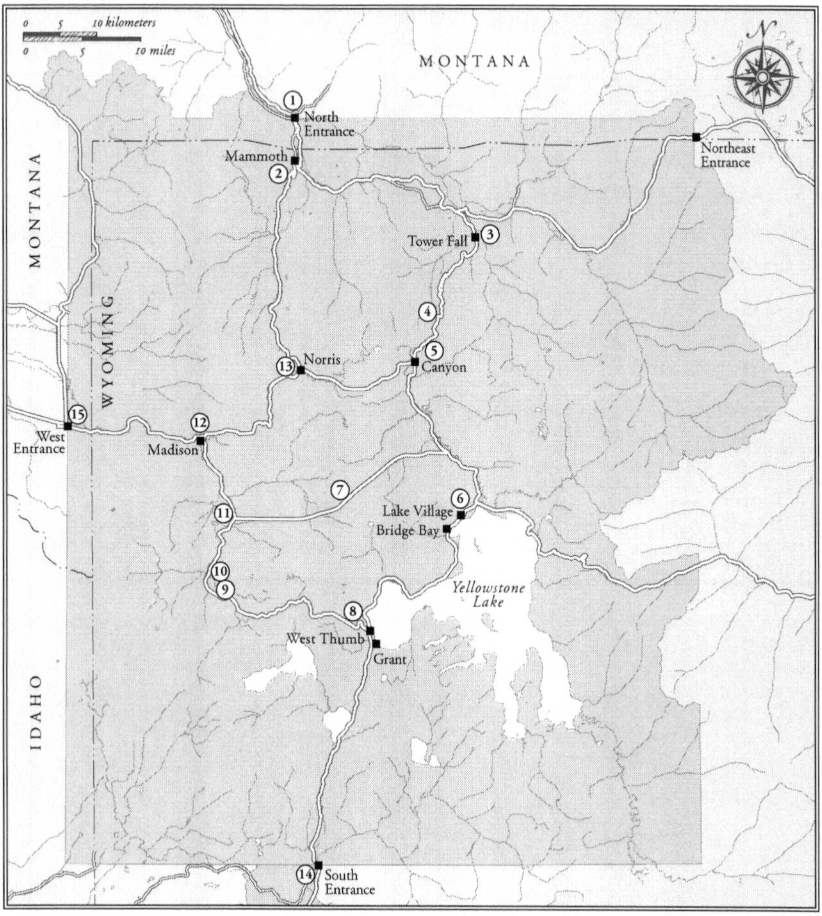
0 5 10 kilometers
0 5 10 miles
MONTANA
MONTANA
WYOMING
IDAHO
North Entrance
Mammoth
Northeast Entrance
Tower Fall
Norris
Canyon
West Entrance
Madison
Lake Village
Bridge Bay
Yellowstone Lake
West Thumb
Grant
South Entrance
1
2
3
4
5
6
7
8
9
10
11
12
13
14
15

Map Legend

1. North Entrance (Gardiner, Montana): In the 1870s travelers reached the North Entrance to Yellowstone Park near the current town of Gardiner by an arduous ride through the Yellowstone River's Yankee Jim Canyon. By 1903 a spur line of the Northern Pacific Railroad was delivering passengers there.

2. Mammoth Hot Springs: Early Yellowstone tourists could either camp near Mammoth Hot Springs or stay at McCartney's Cabin, a crude log cabin with a sod roof that doubled as a hotel. In 1885 the Cottage Hotel was built and it was replaced in 1893 by the National Hotel,

3. Tower Fall: Dramatic rock spires surround this 132-foot fall on Tower Creek. It was a camp spot of early travelers and remains a favorite scenic stop. In 1877 Emma Cowan, who had been released from captivity by the Nez Perce, recognized the fall and felt reassured that she and her siblings would find safety.

4. Mount Washburn: The 10,243-foot mountain is named for General Henry Washburn who led the famous 1870 expedition that brought the Yellowstone Park area to public attention. Its pinnacle provides a grand panorama of 50 miles including Yellowstone Lake.

5. Yellowstone Falls: The Upper Fall (109 feet) and the Lower Fall (308 feet) along with the Grand Canyon of the Yellowstone have always been a highlight of trips to the park.

6. Yellowstone Lake: In 1874 Sarah Tracey and Mabel Cross Osmond took a boat rides on the 136-square-mile Yellowstone Lake.

7. Mary Mountain: The Mary Mountain trail took early tourists between the Lower Geyser Basin and Hayden Valley. Using it required side trips back and forth to see the Upper Geyser Basin and Lake Yellowstone. The route was not used after the Army Corps of Engineers finished roads on the current loop route.

8. West Thumb: This large branch of Lake Yellowstone is where Eleanor Corthell and her family first encountered geothermal features because they came into the park through the Southern Entrance.

9. Upper Geyser Basin: The Upper Geyser Basin is the home of Old Faithful and many other spectacular geysers. Early tourists often camped there for several days to watch the grand geysers play.

10. Midway Geyser Basin: The Midway Geyser Basin was often called "Hell's Half Acre" by early tourists. It was the home of the largest geyser in the world, Excelsior, which threw a column 300 feet wide 300 feet into the air. Now dormant, the Excelsior erupted intermittently in the 1880s and 1990s.

11. Lower Geyser Basin: The first road to Yellowstone's grand geysers ended at the Lower Geyser Basin and in 1880, Marshall's, the park's first hotel, was built there. Carrie Strahorn liked the hotel and befriended its owners, but Margaret Cruickshank condemned it.

12. Madison Junction: At the confluence of the Firehole and Gibbon rivers, Madison Junction was a clear landmark and frequent campsite for early tourists.

13. Norris Geyser Basin: Last of the major geyser basins discovered. Margaret Cruikshank spent a miserable night here in 1883. In 1892 Georgina Synge watched several geysers including a dramatic eruption of the Monarch, which has been dormant since 1913.

14. South Entrance: The army began patrolling the South Entrance to the park in 1892. Eleanor Corthell brought her seven children through this lesser used entrance in 1903.

15. West Entrance (West Yellowstone, Montana): In the 1870s there were no roads across Yellowstone Park so travelers who wanted to see the grand geysers entered through the West Entrance while those who wanted to go to the resort at Mammoth Hot Springs used the North Entrance. Some tourists, like the woman identified only as HWS, came to the West Entrance by team and wagon. The railroad arrived there in 1908.

By the early 1900s most women abandoned sidesaddles and began wearing split skirts so they could ride astride.

PREFACE

I've been interested in stories by adventurous women who visited Yellowstone Park ever since I was a little boy listening to my grandmother's tales of her trip there in 1909. Grandma went with an entourage led by her aunt that included seven of her cousins and two of her brothers. They had a wagon for food and camping equipment, five saddle horses, and a surrey for my great aunt and the small children. The trip took four weeks and they camped out every night.

Grandma bragged about making herself a split riding skirt to ride through the park astride when most women still rode sidesaddle. She told stories about her father and grandfather who went to the park in 1882. One of their favorite tricks, she said, was stealing one another's red flannel underwear and tossing it into a geyser to tint the next eruption red.

Grandma never wrote a complete description of the trip so I began looking for accounts of trips to the park to gain a better understanding of what it must have been like. I have wanted to compile a book of women's tales of their adventures in Yellowstone Park for a long time.

When I got a good collection of women's accounts of their Yellowstone Park travel, I applied to be a member of the Humanities Montana's impressive speakers bureau. Under their auspices I lectured on "Sidesaddles and Geysers" dozens of times all across the state for more than a decade. All that time I was collecting Yellowstone tourists' tales. Recently I decided I had enough truly compelling women's stories for a book.

Sidesaddles and Geysers contains ten of the very best from my collection of more than fifty stories written by women who visited the park. They are arranged chronologically by the date of the trip rather than when they were written or published. The earliest stories are by women who visited the park shortly after it was established in 1872. To get to the park then, tourists might need military escorts to protect them from Indians. And to see the wonders at the interior of the park—falls, lakes, and geysers—they had to ride on horseback through a roadless wilderness. Often it took them several weeks to finish a park tour.

By the time of the latest stories at the dawn of the twentieth century, the Army Corps of Engineers had built some of the best roads in America in the park and women could speed between luxury hotels in comfortable coaches. Others preferred to tour with the more modestly priced permanent camps that provided lodging in tents put up for the summer season. Then there were the "sagebrushers" who preferred the economy and freedom of camping out with their own equipment.

This book includes stories by a wide range of women, some of whom visited the park as children and others who traveled with adult children. There are stories by pioneer women who lived near the park and by those who came from as far away as Great Britain.

The stories have been edited for readability, and grammatical and spelling errors (and foreign spellings) have been corrected. Longer pieces were condensed to focus on dramatic events. When writers offered obsolete and untrue explanations of what they were seeing, I excised them. However, I took care to retain the authors' styles because they convey their personalities and emotions.

Too many people to name have helped me, but I particularly want to thank my lifelong friend Ralph Schmidt, who shared his deep knowledge of Yellowstone Park; Ann Butterfield, who always offered insightful comments and enthusiastic support, and Rachel Phillips, who helped me choose photographs from the Gallatin History Museum collection. Also, thanks to the volunteers at the Gallatin History Museum, especially my fellow members of "The Friday Crew," Ellie Bowles and Helen Backlin.

Finally, I want to thank my wife, Tamara Miller, who leaves me to the hours of solitude that a writer requires, but always offers sound advice when asked.

Frying Doughnuts in Bear Grease

Sarah Tracy—1874

In the spring of 1869 Bozeman pioneer William Tracy went back to Illinois where he courted Sarah Jane Bessie and married her on October 19. The newly-weds returned to Montana by steamboat to Fort Benton and then by team and wagon to Bozeman. As they approached the town William told Sarah to put on her best clothes because men in Bozeman would be waiting to see her—and they were.

Indians stole a band of horses the day before Sarah Tracy left Bozeman for Yellowstone Park in June of 1874. But Mrs. Tracy was used to Indians. When she arrived in Bozeman Indians were encamped on the south side of town. She said, "They would peer in the windows if the doors were locked, or come flocking around the door begging for biscuits, soap, clothes, everything."

Such encounters left Mrs. Tracy with little fear of Indians, but the commander at Fort Ellis, the army post near Bozeman, didn't want to let her party go to Yellowstone in the midst of "Indian troubles." Finally, after some haggling, he agreed to provide an armed escort for part of the way.

Yellowstone Park was just a year old in 1873 and a trip there was a formidable adventure. Only two primitive roads penetrated the edges of the park, one to Mammoth Hot Springs on the north and another to the Lower Geyser Basin on the west. Otherwise the 3,500-square-mile park was a roadless wilderness. Guides, most of them prospectors who had scoured the park looking for gold, hung around McCartney's cabin at Mammoth Hot Springs, offering their services but before long dozens of travelers left the trails obvious so they were no longer needed.

In her reminiscence, Mrs. Tracy notes that the recently constructed road ended at Mammoth Hot Springs and she had to learn how to ride sidesaddle to see the other sites. She and her female companion were taken sailing on Lake Yellowstone and rewarded by being allowed to cook doughnuts in bear grease. Mrs. Tracy's hand-written reminiscence is in the collection of the Museum of the Rockies in Bozeman.

* * * *

1

Early travelers like Sarah Tracy and Mable Cross Osmond cruised Lake Yellowstone on the Sallie, a boat that was built on there. The photo is by Joshua Crissman, a photographer who accompanied Sarah's party on their trip to the park.
COURTESY MUSEUM OF THE ROCKIES.

A trip to the National Park in 1874 was quite a different undertaking than it is today when one can go with as much ease and comfort as can be found in any pleasure trip. In the spring of 1874, a man named Zack Root procured an old stagecoach and, fitting it up with a four-horse team, started a stage and mail route from Bozeman to the Mammoth Hot Springs contracting to carry the mail once a week.

The road was located the same as now. Yankee Jim had built his toll road and collected tolls form all who traveled over it.[1] He had expended a considerable sum of money in making what had been a trail into a wagon road and one could only wonder what is was originally as it fairly made one shudder to ride over it in a four-horse stagecoach. It took two days to make the trip

1 Actually, Yankee Jim George took over the road through the canyon that still bears his name after Bozeman financier Leander Black abandoned it.

2

of seventy miles the night station being Phil Bottler's ranch. A Mrs. Graham and myself were going to the Mammoth Springs to remain a week and then be joined by our husbands and make the tour of the park.

The night before leaving home the Crow Indians made a little stealing escapade in town, coming past the garrisoned fort at Ellis and driving off a band of horses. The alarm was given shortly after midnight and a company of citizens started in pursuit soon to be joined by the soldiers from the fort.

Early in the morning we started with the four-horse stagecoach. When we got to the fort the commanding officers would not let us proceed further on account of the Indian scare. But after some talk the driver asked for an escort which was granted and we were soon on the way with twelve mounted soldiers. Their guns on the shoulder, their belts filled with cartridges, their knapsacks on their shoulders looked war like.

They accompanied us as far as Ferrell's ranch where we stopped at a ranch house for dinner. Seeing no signs of Indians they started back to the fort and we went on to Bottler's for the night.

It is seventy-five miles from Bozeman to the Mammoth Springs and it took two days of good driving as the roads were then. As we neared the springs we climbed a very steep mountain from the summit getting a fine (breath taking) view of the wonderful Mammoth Hot Springs. The descent down the mountains required what was known as rough-locking, fastening the rear wheels with log chains as well as the wagon breaks. This road has not been traveled for many years but there still remain faint traces of the old road coming down the hill where the icehouses now stand.

We drove up to the Hotel with a grand flourish of the four-horse whip bringing the landlord and the guests to the door to meet us. The guests were Mrs. Sanford Ruffner and children, and Miss Williams (now Mr. R. Barnett, Stella Fitzstephens' mother.) The hotel still stands up in the gulch but [is] completely overshadowed by the Grand Mammoth Springs Hotel.

Twenty dollars a week for room and board and five dollars extra for baths was the price. The menu hardly as elaborate or as well served as one now gets in the large hotel. But we enjoyed everything. The baths in the primitive tin bathtubs—nature had coated them over with a beautiful white coating making them to rival the modern porcelain ones. Everything was just as nature made it, unmolested by man. No building but the hotel, store and bathhouses.

We climbed the terraces, explored the natural cave, visited the Devils Kitchen, walked to the river to fish, enjoyed two baths and three hearty meals each day and were ready the next Monday morning to start our horseback ride through the park. When the remainder of our company came there were fifteen persons in our outfit, Mrs. Graham and I being the only ladies. I had never ridden on horseback before so no little difficulty was experienced in selecting the little grey pony that carried one safely through the park. We rode sidesaddle and it was quite difficult for an amateur rider to keep seated. We had eight packhorses, a riding pony for each person, a guide with his packhorses, a photographer with two pack mules.[2] When we were starting out on the trail we made quite an imposing appearance.

Our trail crossed the Gardner River four or five times, a very rapid stream with large boulders at the bottom. I was in great fear in crossing but as there was no alternative I had to hold on as best I could. At first I dismounted to walk over the bad places but they were so frequent I concluded to remain in the saddle. Our old mountaineer remarked, wait until the mountains are so steep that you must hold on to the horse's ears going up and the tail going down. Some mountains where the saddle would slip over the back going up and nearly over the head coming down.

We made only one ride each day, as it was so much work to pack the horses. The guide was the cook and his cooking utensils such were used by the campfire. The baking powder bread was mixed in the mouth of the flower sack, then baked in the frying pan before the campfire. As soon as sufficiently hardened it was taken out and put against a piece of wood while the frying pan was used to cook the bacon.

We had a coffee pot, some tin plates, cups, tin spoons, a few knives and forks. In the morning it was very interesting to watch the men do the packing. None but an experienced mountaineer could pack the horses correctly. A peculiar hitch of the ropes call the "diamond hitch" must be used and to took pilgrims a long time to learn it. The bedding was rolled in canvas, one roll on each side of the packsaddle and must be evenly balanced. Then the valises grips and last of all the kitchen utensils. One staid old horse had the honor of carrying these on top of his pack. One morning soon after leaving camp it slipped down under him and he commenced to buck. On he went bucking at every step scattering knives forks and spoons far and wide. When he was

---

2 The photographer apparently was Joshua Crissman who was known to have gone to the park in 1874.

stopped and we searched and found our implements in a sad condition, both coffee pots jammed so we could hardly use them and many utensils missing.

The trail we followed went first to the Tower Falls, a beautiful fall in the Tower Creek. Our next point of interest was the Grand Canyon and Great Falls of the Yellowstone. We had no fine grade up the mountains to view the Falls but a hard long climb but we felt repaid when we viewed the Great Falls and wonderful canyon. Our trail led around Mount Washburn, the Sulphur Mountain, the mud geysers and then to the Yellowstone Lake.

At the lake we found Commodore Topping and his partners.[3] They had completed a good-sized sailboat. The Commodore was waiting for ladies to ride in his boat, the first ones to name it. As both our names was Sarah we readily agreed to christen the boat "The Sallie." We had a fine sail across the lake and our pictures taken on board after the name was painted on the side. They had a nice camp and gave us the privilege of making some doughnuts and frying them in bears grease.

We then followed a blazed trail across the Upper Geyser Basin. This trail was blazed by Professor Hayden and party sent by the government to make surveys of the country.[4] A blazed trail is where a tree is cut on one side every half mile. We had to depend largely on the sun for direction. We climbed the steepest mountains over fallen timber our horses having to jump across fallen trees. Many times the inexperienced ones would fall off their saddles. That was me and then would all have a good laugh but really only fell off three or four times the entire trip.

The sun clouded in and it commenced raining. We tried to follow the blazed trail but in the pouring rain that followed we got lost entirely. We came toward night to the foot of a very high mountain and made camp, wet through, tired and hungry. I stood by the campfire to dry my clothes. My dress had a long polonaise of calico and when it got dry caught fire and the while back was burned off. We made camp on the wet grounds slept in our wet bedding, awoke refreshed to climb the mountain and got a fine view of the Upper Geyser Basin.

---

3 Eugene Topping and Frank Williams received a permit to operate boats on Yellowstone Lake in 1874 and built one there that summer.

4 Ferdinand Vandiveer led the first government expedition to explore the area that became Yellowstone Park in 1871.

Coming in near Old Faithful we camped a few days to see the grand display, all the natural formations undisturbed by the hand of man. We came down through the Lower Basin. Camped for lunch at the Devils Paint pots as they were then called. We thought them wonderful. Then passed Hells half acre now called The Excelsior Geyser. Then back to Mammoth Springs Hotel.

We were gone twelve days and all thought that bacon and bears' grease doughnuts had certainly agreed with us, and the balmy breezes and the mountain sunshine had done complexions to a turn. While our clothing was a little the worse for wear yet we had seen the Yellowstone National Park in its primitive beauty.

Dolly Saved My Life

Mable Cross Osmond—1874

Mable Cross Osmond was just six and a half years old when she first visited Yellowstone National Park in 1874, and she probably was the first white child to see its interior. Her mother, though not physically strong, was one of the very first non-native women to see Yellowstone's falls, lakes, and geysers.

Mable's father, Captain Robert Cross, was the post trader at Crow Agency, which was located about forty miles east of the nearest town back then, Bozeman, Montana. The trip to the park was through Indian country so Captain Cross arranged for a military escort to the Bottler brothers' ranch in the Paradise Valley south of the current town of Livingston.

Mable offers vivid descriptions of her arduous trip riding up and down steep hills on horseback, creeping to the edges of deep canyons, and walking gingerly around geothermal features. She also captures the excitement of seeing Yellowstone Park's marvelous sights for the first time.

After Mrs. Osmond's first visit to Yellowstone Park in 1874, it was fifty-one years before she returned, but she still had vivid memories of it. Her reminiscence includes such details as the saddle she used to ride on a gentle pony that saved her life. Her second visit inspired the following reminiscence, which is from the Gallatin History Museum.

* * * *

We had gone to Montana in the spring of 1873, my grandfather, Dr. James Wright of Des Moines, Iowa, having been appointed General Superintendent of the Indian Agencies in the Territory of Montana.

He and his family located in Helena, while we went on to the Crow Indian Agency where my father, Captain Robert William Cross, of the 23rd. Iowa Infantry in the recent Civil War, was to be Post Trader. There we were soon joined by Dr. Wright, who had been made agent for the Crows when Congress abolished the office of General Superintendent.

The Crow Agency was then located forty miles east of Bozeman, the nearest town of any kind, and eight miles from the ford of the Yellowstone River. And a very poor location it was, with foothills on two sides, and on another a deep ravine filled with underbrush, all affording an easy approach for attacking bands of Sioux. One month for four Monday nights in succession they fired on us from across the ravine and I recall distinctly the whiz of their bullets over the stockade and also shivering with fear as we hurriedly dressed in the dark—but that is another story.

It was in the summer of 1874 that my father decided on our trip through Yellowstone Park before returning to our home in Des Moines. He had been

McCartney's cabin at Mammoth Hot Springs served as a hotel for Yellowstone Park travelers in the 1870s. It was the only occupied building in the park when Mable Osmond visited there in 1874.
NATIONAL PARK SERVICE.

in the park before while out on a government mission to the Bannocks, but how far he had been, I do not know.

Careful preparations were necessary for our undertaking as it was most unusual for a woman to make the trip and never before had a child been there; at least a white child and not likely an Indian, as they avoided the Geyser country, calling it "bad man's land."[1] I was then six and a half years old. My father had a special saddle made for me—as of course we all rode horseback. The blacksmith, taking a man's saddle, fastened a covered iron rod from the pommel around on the right side to the back. This rod and the seat were well padded with blankets. A covered stirrup, wide enough for my two feet was hung on the left side and across this open side from the pommel to the rod in back was attached a buckled leather strap so that, when mounted, I sat as a child in a high chair.

My dun-colored Indian pony, named "Dolly" was found most trustworthy, saving my life by instantly stopping when, while descending a steep trail my saddle turned, leaving me hanging head downward, helplessly strapped in until the others could reach me. At first my father had a leading rope on her, but after two or three days that was found unnecessary as she followed his horse everywhere, climbing the steepest trails and through the streams, swimming the Yellowstone on our return trip.

On starting one bright morning early in July we rode in an Agency wagon with an armed escort for the first day out. This found to be a wise precaution for the following day on this same road between the Agency and the ford two men were attacked and killed by the Sioux.

That was two years before the Custer battle. I think our first day's ride took us to the Bottler ranch—anyway it was here that our escort turned back after seeing-us over the most dangerous part of the trip. And here we enjoyed one of "Grandma" Bottler's good dinners. I remember the cute little roast pig with an ear of corn in its mouth, and also being awakened during the night by hearing her shrilly shouting, "Fredereek, Fredereek, the skunk is after the chickuns." Though eighty years old, she kept her "store teeth" put away—"fearing to wear them out"—she told us.

---

1 It was a common misconception that Native Americans feared the geothermal features of the area. Archaeological evidence indicates they had lived in the area for 10,000 years. The Sheep Eater Band of the Shoshone frequented the area until the park was established.

Our party consisted of six in all—my father, mother, myself, and two young men, friends of my father's from Bozeman. I think one was named Coleman, and the other was the good old camp cook, who was also a scout. He and my father had attended to the selection of the horses, pack mules and packs, tents, bedding, supplies and cooking utensils, including a Dutch oven, for after leaving Bottler's ranch there was only the wilderness and no food to be secured, except fish and game.

There was at that time no road into the park except from Virginia City and we were entering from the north, so we took to the game and Indian trails. Upon reaching Mammoth Hot Springs we camped in the wooded glen, afterwards most inappropriately named "Chinaman's Gulch," and remained for several days. My father fashioned a basket out of some stays from mother's corset and laid it in one of the pools of the "Terraces," where the waters were constantly running and left it until our return. We found it beautifully encrusted with the mineral deposits. This we took back to Iowa along with an interesting collection of which I still have a few specimens.

We could not travel far each day as my mother was not strong and, unfortunately, had a rough riding horse, not the one selected for her, as it had not come in off the range on the last "roundup." After a day's ride when a camping place had been decided upon, a buffalo robe was quickly unpacked and my father would lift her down onto it. There she would rest while we all got busy. The horses were unsaddled and the pack mules relieved of their burdens so they could all be picketed. The cook having started his camp fire, undid the packs, set up the oven and prepared the bread for baking and then attended to the fish, or game, and the rest of the dinner. Fish were so plentiful that in the small streams the men could straddle from side to side and, leaning down, pick them up in their hands.

In the meantime the two tents had been set up and robes spread for our beds. My first duty was to pick and feed Dolly hands full of the long grass growing so abundantly and she always expected this feast. The days were warm and lovely and the nights were cold! So cold that of mornings the water in the tin washbasin would be frozen from the time one would use it until the next.

One whole day we rode through timber so dense and so tall that we scarcely saw the sky and our horses often had to jump the fallen logs, which nearly covered the ground. The pack mules found it very difficult to get through and one big mule, named Ben, would even get down on his knees to squeeze between the trees.

At the Upper Geyser Basin we remained several days waiting to see the Giantess in eruption. One night it was surely expected, so a big fire was built of logs. Robes spread, we watched for several hours. The crater filled and refilled to the brim several times, but it was not until the next afternoon that the eruption commenced. We were in camp some distance away at the edge of the timber. My father, who was off riding, came galloping to camp to tell us. There were no roads, or signs of any kind to give warning, so as he rode across the crusty formation, his horse broke through. He jumped off his horse fortunately striking firm ground and jerked his horse after him. When he looked back down the hole, he could see no bottom.

Of course we watched old Faithful several times and collected some of the small, smooth pebbles which fell with the water into the pools. One time, the wind veering quickly, my mother was slightly burned by the hot water that struck her arm and shoulder.

One delightful and unusual experience we had there was of the meeting of a small party of people who came from Virginia City, including Mr. Fuller, I think his name was, and his talented daughter, who was soon returning East to finish her musical education. She sang for us as we sat around the campfire and it was wonderfully impressive in that vast solitude. These were apparently the only other humans in the park, except for two trappers at the lake.

It has always seemed to me that from the geysers we went on to Yellowstone Lake and the Falls and then over Mount Washburn to Tower Creek Falls and then back to Mammoth Hot Springs, but I may be mistaken as to the order of our journey.

Anyway, we went to Yellowstone Lake and camped on the shore with two men who claimed to be government trappers. They had a small sailboat and took us for a ride to a small island where we found delicious ripe red raspberries and gooseberries. Nothing ever tasted better. I recall on returning, the lake was rough and there was considerable "tacking" necessary, and much rocking of the boat so I became quite seasick.

The trappers named one island "Mable's Island" in my honor, as I was the first child there.[2] I recall passing Sulphur Mountain somewhere along the way and of my father getting a specimen.

---

2 The name didn't take.

While visiting the Falls, we went out onto the ledge overlooking the Lower Falls. After fastening one end of a long rope to a tree and the other end around his waist, my father carried me onto the ledge. I remember my mother remaining farther back with closed eyes.

Crossing Mount Washburn we saw our only bear, a black one. My father took a shot at it, but it ran into the Woods. We also saw way off in a valley, a large herd of buffalo.

At Tower Falls we climbed down and stood back of that big boulder. It was here that my mother came near a serious accident. She was climbing down ahead of us holding to a branch, which gave way and she slid down some distance before a tree fortunately stopped her. We returned to Mammoth Hot Springs and then over the trail northward and across the Yellowstone River to the Crow Agency.

It was on our way out that we encountered our only sight of Indians being near by. I can still feel a thrill as we caught sight of a dog on the crest of a hill ahead of US. A dog in that wilderness meant Indians were near. The men hastily unslung their guns—their braces of pistols and belt of

The descent to the base of the Lower Falls of the Yellowstone was arduous before a stairway was installed.
NATIONAL PARK SERVICE.

cartridges they always wore—and proceeded cautiously up the trail, but when we reached the top of the hill, the dog was gone. My father never seemed to fear the Indians, but my mother was always deadly afraid of them, even our own friendly Crows.

I remember my father saying we were twenty-four days in the saddle, riding about 550 miles.

That fall we returned to Des Moines, Iowa, and though in later years we lived in Utah, I was never in the park again until the summer of 1925, when I recalled two of our camping places and remembered many of the sights.

Captured by Indians

Emma Cowan—1877

Emma Cowan and her family visited Yellowstone National Park in 1877—the year the U.S. Army pursued the Nez Perce Indians through the park. The Nez Perce generally had amicable relations with whites, but in what has become a familiar story, the peace was shattered when gold was discovered on Indian land. Some Nez Perce acquiesced to government demands to move to a tiny reservation, but others decided to flee their homeland instead.

The Army sent soldiers to subdue the defiant Nez Perce, but the Indians defeated them several times. In the most dramatic battle, the Army made a predawn attack on the sleeping Nez Perce camp on the banks of the Big Hole River in southwest Montana. The Nez Perce rallied, drove back their attackers, then retreated, leaving their equipment, teepees, and at least 89 dead—many of them women and children.

After the battle they fled through Yellowstone Park, an unexpected move because people thought Indians feared the geysers. After making their way through the rugged Yellowstone wilderness, the Nez Perce discovered they were not welcome with their old friends the Crow, who had made an accommodation with the whites. Then they headed north hoping to join Sitting Bull and his Sioux in Canada. In October the starving and exhausted remnants of the band surrendered to the Army just 40 miles from the Canadian border.

Nez Perce took Emma and her brother and sister captive, and shot her husband George three times. George survived and kept the bullet an army surgeon dug out of his head as a watch fob for the rest of his life.

Despite her ordeal, Emma was sympathetic to the plight of the Nez Perce. She published her account of her trip twenty-five years after the events of the summer of 1877, so it's not surprising that she misremembered some details. Still it is a marvelous account of her adventures.

Critics consider Emma Cowan's memoir one of the gems of Montana litera-ture. It was originally published in 1903 in Contributions to Historical Society of Montana *and has been republished many times. Here is a condensed version.*

* * * *

In Virginia City, where we lived the first year in Montana, 1864-1865, my father one day brought home an old man who told us some very marvelous stories.[1] My father termed them fish stories, however, I enjoyed them immensely. My fairy books could not equal such wonderful tales—fountains of boiling water, crystal clear, thrown hundreds of feet in the air, only to fall back into cups of their own forming—pools of water within whose limpid depths tints of the various rainbows were reflected—mounds and terraces of gaily colored sand—these and many others were the tales unfolded.

Though the old man might have been rough and uncultured, he seemed to have an innate appreciation of the beautiful in nature. He told of the beauties of the now National Park, though never a work of that which savors somewhat of the uncanny, the hot mud and sulphur. I fancy he dared not, lest we should consider him daft. He told us much that is familiar to those who have since visited the geysers, a region in those years unknown.

Although we enjoyed his stories, for he told them well, we considered them merely the fantasy of his imagination. Still I gleaned from them my first impression of Wonderland. As I grew older and found truth in the statements, the desire to someday visit this land was ever present.

In 1875 I was married, and in 1877 occurred our memorable trip to the park and capture by the Nez Perce Indians. We were told that the Indian is superstitious. The phenomena of the geysers very probably accounts for the fact that this land is not now and never has been Indian country. A few Indian trails are found within the boundaries of the park as they are in other parts of the West. Yet this year the Indians were very much in evidence in the national park, as we found to our sorrow.

We were thankful, however, that it was the Nez Perce we encountered, rather than a more hostile tribe, as they were partially civilized and generally peaceful. Yet at this day, knowing something of the circumstances that led to the final outbreak and uprising of these Indians, I wonder that any of us were spared. Truly a quality of mercy was shown us during our captivity that

---

1 The man must have been Gilman Sawtell who settled at Henrys Lake, Idaho, and harvested fish there to sell in Montana gold camps.

George and Emma Cowan returned to Yellowstone Park in 1901. They are shown with their family at the site of the couple's 1877 encounter with the Nez Perce.
GALLATIN HISTORY MUSEUM.

a Christian might emulate, and at that time when they must have hated the very name of the white race.

Deprived of their reservation, on which they had lived years without number, and because they rebelled and refused to sign a treaty giving up the last remnant of this land, hunted and hounded and brought to battle, wounded and desperate, fleeing with their wives and children to any land where the white man was not—yet they were kind to us, a handful of the hated oppressors. Think of it, you who assume to be civilized people! Less than ten days had elapsed since the Big Hole fight in Montana, in which women and children, as well as warriors, were killed by the score. A number, badly wounded, were in camp while we were there. Yet were we treated kindly, given food and horses, and sent to our homes.

The summer of 1877 was exceedingly hot and dry. This together with a grasshopper raid, which was not the least of the trials of the pioneer, made the necessity of closing up the house to keep out the pests almost unbearable.

My brother Frank told us of his intention to visit the park, and asked us to be in the party. It required but little effort on his part to enthuse us, and we soon began preparations for the trip.

Several people from our town Radersburg talked also of going, but by the time we were ready, one acquaintance only, Mr. Charles Mann, joined our party, from that town.

I induced my mother to allow my young sister, a child of little more than a dozen years, to accompany me, as I was to be the only woman in the party and she would be so much company for me.

The party consisted all told of the following persons: A. J. Arnold, J. A. Oldham and a Mr. Dingee, all of Helena, Mr. Charles Mann, my brother Frank Carpenter, Mr. Cowan, my sister, myself, and a cook named Myers.

We were nicely outfitted with an easy double-seated carriage, baggage wagon and four saddle horses, one of them my own pony, a birthday gift from my father years before, which I named Bird because she was trim and fleet. That I was fond of her goes without saying. We were well equipped in the way of provisions, tents, guns, and last, but not least, musical instruments. With J. A. Oldham as violinist, my brother's guitar, and two or three fair voices, we anticipated no end of pleasure.

We left Radersburg the sixth of August, camping the first night at Three Forks. Our way lay up the Madison via Henry's Lake, a road having been built to the Lower Geyser Basin from that direction. Although some parts of this would scarcely pass as a road, we traveled it without mishap. The second day's ride brought us to Sterling, a small town in Madison County and a pleasant one. But as night approached, we were still some miles from town. Leaving our slower baggage wagon, we pushed on, reaching town after dark. As we could not camp until the wagon came, we went to the hotel for supper, and made camp later. Several of the townspeople joined us there, and we heard for the first time rumors of Indian trouble. Some advised us not to go farther, but we did not think it more than an old time Indian scare, and when morning came, bright and beautiful, we decided to go on our way. Often with night, I would feel somewhat timid, but with the daylight my fears would be dispelled.

The next noon found us at Ennis, and twelve miles farther up the Madison for our night camp. We passed the last of the ranches that afternoon. At

Ennis my husband had been told we would find fishing at Henry's Lake, also boats, spears, skeins and all sorts of tackle. The man, to whom they belonged, however, was at one of the ranches cutting hay, but he would give us a key to the boathouse if we could find him. Inquiring at the ranch to which we had been directed, we found that he had gone to another, five miles distant. My disappointment may be imagined for my fancy had run riot and I fully expected to see the old man of the tales of my childhood. A horseback ride a few miles obtained the key, but my curiosity was not gratified then or afterwards.

In the afternoon two days later we left the Madison River, up which we had been traveling, and crossed a low divide, getting our first glimpse of the lake.[2] The view from this point is exceedingly pretty. Some of the pleasantest days of our trip were spent here. Innumerable flocks of wild fowl have their home in this isolated spot. Low marshy land encircles the greater part of this lake, but where the houses are built the ground is much higher, giving a fine view of the lake and surrounding hills. The immense spring affords a sufficient stream of water to float a boat through the marsh and out to the lake.

Torchlight fishing by night was a unique pastime. Great schools of fish, attracted by the glare of light from blazing pine knots gathered about the prow of the boat. Some fine ones were speared and delicious meals enjoyed.

Nothing quite equals the fine salmon trout unless it may be venison steak or the perfectly delicious grouse, the thought of which sets my heart longing for the breezy pine-capped hills and mountain stream.

On a summer day Mr. Cowan and I mounted our horses in search of large game, to-wit: the venison steak. But though we spent the entire day in the saddle, ranging over the hills and gulches, we found not a track. At Sunday we returned to camp, only to find it deserted. The others of the party had planned to cross the lake and explore Snake River, which has its source in Henry Lake. They had not yet returned and we could see nothing of them. The day, which had been lovely, changed with the setting of the sun.

Great banks of clouds came scurrying across the sky. the soughing of the wind through the pines brought the thought of storm, the darkness was

2 The party was going over Raynolds Pass, which crosses the Continental Divide between Idaho and Montana. This route required the party to cross the divide again over Targhee Pass to reach Yellowstone Park, but it was the easiest route at the time.

coming rapidly and the day ending drearily. I was in a fever of anxiety, feeling sure some accident had befallen them. We made a great bonfire, and not long afterward there came a faint hello from across the water, a most welcome sound. A long half hour elapsed then before they reached camp, tired but jolly. A strong head wind and broken oar had made it all but impossible to land. A rousing fire, good supper, comparing notes, telling stories, singing songs, ended a long remembered day.

The following morning we broke camp and continued our travel. We passed to the southeast and crossed Targhee Pass, then through ten miles of pine barrens, and camped again on the Madison River at the mouth of the canyon. Some nineteen times we crossed the river in traveling through the canyon. Fortunately, the water was low, so we had no trouble on that score. The road was very dim, however, and the men rode in advance. As they passed out of the stream they would tie a white cloth to a brush or bough, thus indicating just where to ford. Some very picturesque scenery is found along this route. Flowers grew in profusion, many varieties I had not found elsewhere.

Our last camp before reaching the Lower Basin was at the junction of the Gibbon and Firehole rivers, these two forming the Madison.

We caught some delicious speckled trout here, our last good fishing grounds. The appetite of the crowd by this time was something appalling, or so the cook seemed to think. At the present time a strike would have been in order. As it was, he could only shirk. We all assisted with the work, which soon meant doing the greater part of it. However, we were good campers and not inclined to grumble. We are in fine health and enjoying the outdoor life to the utmost. We seemed to be in a world of our own.

Not a soul had we seen save our own party, and neither mail nor news of any sort had reached us since leaving the ranches on the Madison.[3]

Leaving the Gibbon fork after dinner, we traveled several miles of low foothills and entered the Lower Geyser Basin. We had at last reached Wonderland. Mr. Cowan insisted always on making camp before doing anything else, putting up tents, gathering fragrant pine bows for camp beds, getting things in regular housekeeping order. But this day our first sight of the geysers—with columns of steam rising from innumerable vents and the smell of

---

3 Emma Cowan's brother, Frank Carpenter, said the party met two prospectors named Hicks and Woods on Targhee Pass. The pair was never heard from again, perhaps killed by the Nez Perce.

the inferno in the air from the numerous sulphur springs—made us simply wild with the eagerness of seeing all things at once.

We left the teams, which, by the way, entered no protest, being worn out by the long travel, and we ran and shouted and called to each other to see this or that, so that we soon became separated and knew it not.

My small sister and I could scarcely keep pace with the men, but we found enough to interest us, turn where we would. I recalled and told to her many of the tales told me of this weird land in earlier years. How vividly they came to mind!

As we wandered about we found some things that were curious, but not altogether pleasant. Among them was a dark depression, full of mud as

These couples have stopped their carriages at the Lower Geyser Basin to enjoy the view.
GALLATIN HISTORY MUSEUM.

thick as hasty pudding, that bubbled and spluttered and popped with a loud explosion. A stick thrown in was quickly sucked out of sight, and the fate of a human being falling in could easily be imagined. It gave one a creepy feeling. At length, as it was nearly sundown and some distance from where we had left the teams, we deemed it best to retrace our steps. We were hungry and tired, but altogether happy. We had realized our expectations. Our camp that night was not quite up to the standard, but no complaints were entered.

The next day we established a permanent camp near the Fountain Geyser, and made daily short excursions to the different points of interest. We explored every nook and cranny of the Lower Basin and were ready for pastures new.

We had reached the terminus of the wagon road but trails led in various directions, one to the Upper Geyser Basin, another to the Falls and Yellowstone lake by way of Mary's Lake.

As we could go no farther with the wagon, we decided to leave our camp intact, only taking the few things necessary for a few days' stay in the Upper Basin, and go horseback. This we did, and pitched our tent that night in a point of timber, very close to Castle Geyser, which by way of reception gave us a night eruption, covering us with spray and making a most unearthly noise.

I was sure the earth would be rent asunder and we would be swallowed up. At night, with our heads pillowed on the breast of Mother Earth, it seemed in close proximity to Dante's Inferno. I think his spirit must have visited the park in some remote age for inspiration.

At dawn we circled around the crater, too late to see more than great columns of steam. We saw the geyser in eruption several times while in the basin, but by daylight it did not seem so terrifying. The Giantess was not in eruption during our stay of five days. We enjoyed the Grand, considering it rightly named. In the meantime, my brother, with some others in the party, had gone to the Falls and Yellowstone Lake. We remained five days in the Upper Basin and arranged to meet the others on the 22nd in the Lower Basin.

Thursday, the 23rd of August, found us all at the home camp, as we termed it, ready to retrace our steps towards civilization. We had a delightful time, but were ready for home. This day we encountered the first and only party of tourists we had seen, General Sherman and party.[4] They had come into the park by way of Mammoth Hot Springs. Of them we learned of the Nez Perce raid and the Big Hole fight.[5] We also received the very unpleasant impression that we might meet the Indians before we reached home.

No one seemed to know just where they were going. The scout who was with the General's party assured us we would be perfectly safe if we would remain in the basin, as the Indians would never come into the park. I observed, however, that his party preferred being elsewhere, as they left the basin that same night.

That afternoon another visitor called at camp, an old man by the name of Shively, who was traveling from the Black Hills and was camped half a mile down the valley. Home seemed a very desirable place just at this particular time, and we decided with one accord to break camp in the morning, with a view of reaching home as soon as possible. Naturally we felt somewhat depressed and worried over the news received.

My brother Frank, and Al Oldham, in order to enliven us somewhat, sang songs, told jokes, and finally dressed up as brigands, with pistols, knives and guns strapped on them. Al Oldham, with his swart complexion, wearing a broad sombrero, looked a typical one, showing off to good advantage before the glaring campfire. They made the woods ring with their nonsense and merriment for some time.

We probably would not have been so serene, had we known that the larger part of the audience consisted of the Indians, who were lurking out in the darkness, watching and probably enjoying the fun.

The advance party of Indians had come into the basin early in the evening. Before morning the entire Indian encampment was within a mile of us, and we had not heard an unusual sound, though I for one slept lightly.[6]

---

4 Emma makes two mistakes here. First, the party had encountered two prospectors named Hicks and Woods while crossing Targhee Pass and a party of tourists led by Yellowstone Pioneer George Huston at the Lower Geyser Basin. Second, General William Tecumseh Sherman had finished his tour of the park and was on his way between Mammoth Hot Springs and Bozeman on this date. The party Emma mentions was probably one led by Bozeman businessman Nelson Story.

5 Emma's brother, Frank Carpenter, says the Radersburg party learned about the Big Hole Battle from Yellowstone Pioneer George Huston.

6 The Radersburg party's bonfire was seen by a young Nez Perce named Yellow Wolf. He and his companions accosted the party the next morning.

I was already awake when the men began building the campfire, and I heard the first guttural tones of two or three Indians who suddenly stood by the fire. I peeped out through the flap of the tent, although I was sure they were Indians before I looked. I immediately aroused my husband, who was soon out. They pretended to be friendly, but talked little.

After some consultation the men decided to break camp at once and attempted to move out as though nothing unusual was at hand. No one cared for breakfast save the Indians, who quickly devoured everything that was prepared. By this time twenty or thirty Indians were about the camp, and more coming. The woods seemed full of them.

Some little time was required to pull down tents, load the wagons, harness and saddle horses, and make ready to travel. While Mr. Cowan was engaged elsewhere one of the men—Mr. Arnold, I think—began dealing out sugar and flour to the Indians on their demand. My husband soon observed this and peremptorily ordered the Indians away, not very mildly either. Naturally they resented it, and I think this materially lessened his chances to escape.

So much ammunition had been used on the trip, especially at Henry Lake, that the supply was practically exhausted. Mr. Cowan had five cartridges only, about ten all told in the party. It was a fortunate thing probably that we had no more, for had the men been well armed, they would have attempted a defense, which could only have ended disastrously to us. Six men arrayed against several hundred Indians splendidly armed would not have survived long.

We drove out finally on the home trail, escorted by forty or fifty Indians. In fact they all seemed to be going our way except the women's camp, which we met and passed as they were traveling up the Firehole towards Mary's Lake. A mile or more was traveled in this way, when the Indians for some reason called a halt. We were then a few hundred yards from where the road enters the timber and ascends the hillside.

One of the Indians seated on a horse near Mr. Cowan, who was also on horseback, raised his hand and voice, apparently giving some commands, for immediately forty or fifty Indians came out of the line of timber, where they evidently had been in ambush for our benefit. Another Indian addressing Mr. Cowan was pointing to the Indian who had given the command, said in good English, "Him Joseph."[7] And this was our introduction to that chief.

---

7 The Nez Perce were probably teasing the tourists. Thee voice overheard was most likely Poker Joe, the chief of a small band. Poker Joe was leading the combined bands through Yellowstone Park.

Every Indian carried a splendid gun, with belts full of cartridges. As the morning sunshine glinted on the polished surface of the gun barrels a regiment of soldiers could have not looked more formidable. We were told to backtrack, which we did, not without some protest, realizing however the utter futility. The Indians pretended all the while to be our very good friends, saying that if they should let us go, bad Indians, as they termed them, would kill us.

Passing and leaving our morning camp to the right, we traversed the trail towards Mary's Lake for two miles. We could go no farther with the wagons on account of fallen timber. Here we unhitched, mounted the horses, taking from the wagon the few things in the way of wraps that we could carry conveniently, and moved on.

It gave us no pleasure to see our wagons overhauled, ransacked and destroyed. Spokes were cut from the buggy wheels and used as whip handles. We did not appreciate the fact that the Indians seemed to enjoy the confiscated property. One young chap dashed past us with several yards of pink mosquito bar tied to his horse's tail. A fine strip of swans down, a trophy from Henry Lake, which an ugly old Indian had wrapped around his head turban fashion, did not please me either.

After traveling some ten miles, a noon camp was made, fires lighted and dinner prepared. Poker Joe acted as interpreter. He talked good English, as could all of them when they desired. Through him we were told that if we would give up our horses and saddles for others that would be good enough to take us home, they would release us and we would be allowed to return to the settlements without harm. Many of their horses were worn out from the long hurried march. Under the circumstances we acquiesced, and an exchange began.

I was seated on my pony, watching the proceedings, when I observed that two or three Indians were gathering around me, apparently admiring my horse, also gently leading her away from the rest of the party. They evidently wanted the animal and I immediately slipped out of the saddle to the ground, knowing that I would never see my pony again, and went to where Mr. Cowan was being persuaded that an old rackabone gray horse was a fair exchange for his fine mount. He was persuaded.

Poker Joe, mounted on my husband's horse, made his circle of the camp, shouting in a sonorous voice some command relative to the march apparently, as the women soon began moving. He came to us finally and told us we could go. We lost no time in obeying the order.

All went well for us for a half-mile or so. Then to our dismay we discovered Indians following us. They soon came up and said the chief wanted to see us again. Back we turned, passed the noon camp, now deserted, and up and on to higher timbered ground. The pallor of my husband's face told me he thought our danger great.

Suddenly, without warning, shots rang out. Two Indians came dashing down the trail in front of us. My husband was getting off his horse. I wondered what the reason. I soon knew, for he fell as soon as he reached the ground—fell heading down hill. Shots followed and Indian yells, and all was confusion.

In less time than it takes to tell it, I was off my horse and by my husband's side, where he lay against a fallen pine tree. I heard my sister's screams and called to her. She came and crouched by me, as I knelt by his side. I saw he was wounded in the leg above the knee, and by the way the blood spurted out I feared an artery had been severed. He asked for water. I dared not leave him to get it, even had it been near.

I think we both glanced up the hill at the same moment, for he said, "Keep quiet. It won't last long." That thought had flashed through my mind also. Every gun in the whole party of Indians was leveled at us three. I shall never forget the picture, which left an impression that years cannot efface. The holes in those gun barrels looked as big as saucers.

I gave it only a glance, for my attention was drawn to something near at hand. A pressure on my shoulder was drawing me away from my husband. Looking back over my shoulder, I saw an Indian with an immense navy pistol trying to get a shot at my husband's head. Wrenching my arm from his grasp, I leaned over my husband, only to be roughly drawn aside. Another Indian stepped up, a pistol shot rang out, my husband's head fell back, and a red stream trickled down his face from beneath his hat. The warm sunshine, the smell of blood, the horror of it all, a faint remembrance of seeing rocks thrown at his head, my sister's screams, a faint sick feeling, and all was blank.

After coming to my senses my first recollection was of a great variety of noises—hooting, yelling, neighing of horses—all jumbled together. For a while it seemed far off. I became conscious finally that someone was calling my name, and I tried to answer. Presently my brother rode close to me. He told me later that I looked years older and that I was ghastly white. He tried to comfort me and said the Indians had told him no further harm would befall us. It seemed to me the assurance had come too late. I could see nothing but my husband's dead face with the blood upon it. I remember Frank's telling me my sister was safe, but it seemed not to impress me much at the time.

The Indians soon learned that my brother was familiar with the trail, and he was sent forward. Over this mountain range, almost impassable because of thick timber, several hundred head of loose horses, packhorses, camp accouterments, and five or six hundred Indians were trying to force a passage.

A narrow trail had sufficed for tourists. It was a feat few white people had accomplished without axe of implements of some sort to cut the way. It required constant watching to prevent loose horses from straying away. As it was, many were lost. The pack animals also caused trouble, often getting wedged between trees. An old woman would pound them on the head until they backed out. And such yelling! Their lungs seemed in excellent condition.

The wearisome uphill travel was at length accomplished. Beyond the summit the timber was less dense, with open glades and parks. Finally, at dusk we came to a quiet valley, which had already begun to glow with campfires, though many were not lighted until sometime later. The Indian who was leading my horse—for I had been allowed to ride alone after recovering consciousness, the Indian retaining a grip on the bridle—threaded his way past numerous camp fires and finally stopped near one.

As if by a pre-arranged plan someone came to the horse, enveloped in a blanket. Until he spoke I thought it to be an Indian, and I was clasped in the arms of my brother. Tears then, the first in all these dreary hours, came to my relief. He led me to the fire and spoke to an Indian seated there, who I was told was Chief Joseph.

He did not speak, but motioned me to sit down. Frank spread a blanket on the ground, and I sat down on it, thoroughly exhausted. A number of women about the fire were getting supper. My first question had been for my sister. I was told that she was at Poker Joe's camp, some little distance away, together with the old man Shively, who was captured the evening before.

I was told I could see her in the morning, and with this assurance I had to be satisfied. Food was offered me, but I could not eat.

My brother and I sat out a weary vigil with Chief Joseph, but without avail. The chief sat by the dying embers of the campfire, somber and silent, foreseeing his gloomy meditations possibly the unhappy ending of his campaign. The "noble red man" we read of was more nearly impersonated in this Indian than in any I have ever met. Grave and dignified, he looked a chief.

A woman sat down near me with a babe in her arms. My brother, wishing to conciliate them, I suppose, lifted it up and placed it in my lap. I glanced at the chief and saw the glimmer of a smile on his face, showing that he had heart beneath that stony exterior. The woman was all smiles, showing her white teeth. Seeing that I was crying, the woman seemed troubled and said to my brother, "Why cry?" He told her my husband had been killed that day. She replied "She heartsick." I was indeed.

The Indians were without tepees, which had been abandoned in the flight from the Big Hole fight, but pieces of canvas were stretched over a pole or bush, thus affording some protections from the cold night air. My brother and I sat out a weary vigil by the dying embers of the campfire sadly wondering what the coming day would bring forth. The Indian who had befriended him told him we would be liberated and sent home. But they had assured us a safe retreat the day previous and had not kept faith. Near morning, rain began falling. A woman arose, replenished the fire, and then came and spread a piece of canvas across my shoulders to keep off the dampness.

At dawn, the fires were lighted, and soon all was activity, and breakfast under way. Some bread, yellow with soda, and willow tea were offered me, but I was not yet hungry. Poker Joe came up and offered to take me to my sister. Frank was told to remain in at the camp for the present, and I clasped his hand, not knowing if I should see him again.

Only a short distance away, which I would have walked gladly the night before, I found my sister. Such a forlorn child I trust I may never again see. She threw herself into my arms in a very paroxysm of joy. She seemed not to be quite certain that I was alive, even though she had been told.

Mr. Shively, the old man before referred to, was at this camp, and I was as glad to see him as though I had known him always. He gave us much encouragement. The Indians had talked more freely to him and he had tried to impress upon them the wisdom of releasing us, telling them we had lived many years in the West and had many friends and that it would be to their advantage to let us go.

Poker Joe again made the circle of the camp, giving orders for the day's march. We were furnished horses and my brother came up leading them that morning. The four of us rode together. We reached the crossing of the Yellowstone near the mud geysers at noon. The Indians plunged into the stream without paying much regard to the regular ford, and camped on the opposite shore.... We watched the fording for some time, and finally crossed.

At the camp dinner was being prepared. I began to feel faint from lack of food. I forced down a little bread, but nothing more. Fish was offered me, but I declined with thanks. I had watched the women prepare them something this wise. From a great string of fish the largest were selected, cut in two, dumped into an immense camp-kettle filled with water, and boiled to a pulp. The formality of cleaning had not entered into the formula. While I admit that tastes differ, I prefer having them dressed.

A council was being held. We were seated in the shade of some trees watching proceedings. Six or seven Indians, the only ones who seemed to be in camp at the time, sat in a circle and passed a long pipe to one to the other. Each took a few whiffs of smoke, and then one by one they arose and spoke. Poker Joe interpreted for us. Presently he said the Indians had decided to let my sister and me go together with the soldier who had been captured that morning, but would hold my brother and Shively for guides. I had not been favorably impressed by the soldier. Intuition told me he was not trustworthy, and I refused to go unless my brother was also released. This caused another discussion, but they agreed to it, and preparations were made for our departure. A search was made for my saddle, but without avail. It was later found by some of Howard's soldiers near where Mr. Cowan was shot.

Some of our bedding, a waterproof tarp, a jacket for my sister, bread and matches and two old worm-out horses were brought, and we were ready. We clasped hands sadly with our good friend Shively, promising to deliver some messages to friends in Philipsburg, should we escape. His eyes were dim with tears. In reality, I considered his chances to escape better than ours and so told him. The Indians needed him for a guide. "We may be intercepted by warriors out of camp," I said. "No," he replied, "something tells me you will get out safely."

We crossed the river again, my brother riding behind Poker Joe, who went with us a half-mile or more, showing us presently a well-defined trail down the river. He told us we must ride, "All night. All day. No sleep." We could reach Bozeman on the second day. He reiterated again and again that we must ride all night. We shook hands and set out very rapidly. My brother walked and the horses we rode were worn out. It seemed folly to think we could escape. Furthermore, we placed no confidence in the Indian. I regret to say that as soon as he was out of sight we left the river trail and skirted along in the timber.

After several miles of travel in this way, we came to a valley through which we must pass to reach the trail down by the falls. We decided to wait on a timbered knoll overlooking the valley until the darkest part of the night, so that we might cross without being seen by the Indians. The moonlight was so bright that it was two o'clock or more before we attempted it. After crossing nearly half way, we came to a washout or cut, over which we could not jump the horses. It seemed to me hours before we finally came to a place where we could cross, so that before we gained the shelter of the timber once more, it was broad daylight.

We passed down the river, leaving to our left the mountain pass over which the Indians had brought us the day before. We dared not retrace that route, even though my husband lay dead there—dead and unburied, perhaps dragged and torn by wild beasts. My own peril seemed of little consequence, compared to the cruel agony of this thought. We passed the falls. I was familiar with the route from this point.[8] I was sure we would find friends nearer than Bozeman, as Poker Joe had said. We would find them at the Mammoth Hot Springs.

About noon the sign that someone was ahead of us was apparent. In crossing streams, pony tracks in the wet sand were plainly seen, and the marks of rope or lasso that had been dragged in the dust of the trail indicated Indians. They often drag the rope thus, I am told.

We passed Tower Creek and stopped a very short time to rest the horses. A few hours later, in rounding a point of timber, we saw in a little meadow not far beyond, a number of horses and men. At first glance we thought them Indians. Frank drew our horses back into the timber and went forward to investigate. He returned in a very few minutes and declared them soldiers. Oh, such a feeling of relief!

---

8 Emma had visited the park in 1874 and traveled to Tower Fall then.

Imagine their surprise when we rode into the camp and my brother told them we were fleeing from the Indians, the only survivors of our party, as he believed then. The soldier we had left at the Nez Perce camp the day before was a deserter from this company.[9] Retribution closely followed transgression in his case. Mr. Shively escaped after being with the Indians ten days, but the fate of the soldier we did not learn.

The company of soldiers was a detachment from Fort Ellis, with Lieutenant Schofield in command. They were sent out to ascertain the whereabouts of the Nez Perce and were returning in belief that the Indians were not in that vicinity. Of them we learned that General Howard was closely following the Indians. Many of their actions were thus accounted for.

The soldiers kindly prepared supper for us. I remember being nearly famished. Camp had been made for the night, but was quickly abandoned, and arrangements made for quick travel. We were mounted on good horses, and the poor old ones that had done us good service, notwithstanding their condition, were turned out to graze to their heart's content.

This night, unlike the previous one, was dark and cloudy. We passed over some of the roughest mountain trails that I ever remembered traveling. Many of the soldiers walked and led their horses. Near midnight we reached Mammoth Hot Springs, tired and stiff from long riding, but truly thankful for our escape.

I found, as I anticipated, some acquaintances, and strangers as well as friends who did everything possible for our comfort. Two Englishmen with their guide were about to make a tour of the park. One of these men was a physician and kindly assisted in dressing wounds. I am certain he never found a time when his services were more appreciated.

A semi-weekly stage had been run to the springs that season. We were told that if we desired we could rest till Wednesday and return to Bozeman on that stage. On Monday, Mr. Calfee invited us to go to Bozeman with him. He said he had a pair of wild mules and a big wagon, but if we wished, he would take us. We were anxious to get home and very glad for so good an opportunity. The Englishman and his guide also decided to return to Bozeman. Wonderland had lost its attractions for the nonce.

---

9 Emma is mistaken here. The soldier was James Irwin who had mustered out of the army at Fort Ellis.

A long day's ride brought us to the Bottler ranch on the Yellowstone. Mr. Calfee decided to remain there a day or so. His photographic supplies were somewhat shaken, likewise his passengers. We found excitement rife at this point. Chief Joseph and his band were expected to raid every section of Montana at the same moment apparently. The Crow Indians, whose reservation is just across the Yellowstone River, extending miles up and down, took advantage of this fact, and numerous horse-stealing raids occurred, for which the Nez Perce received credit.

In the afternoon of the next day a friend drove out from Bozeman, and we made twelve of the forty-mile drive that evening, remaining in the Ferrill home on Trail Creek all night. They received us kindly, and though their own family was large, they made room for us. A sitting room was converted to a bedroom, and camp beds made down for several children.

During the evening we gave them the details of our encounter with the Indians. To them, Indian scares, were common. Living so close to the Crow reservation, they were always on the alert and never felt quite safe. The children listened with great interest, telling us afterward what they would do, should they be captured. They knew where to dig for camas root, and they would escape to the brush and live on that.

We had only gotten settled for the night when a neighbor came tapping at the door, telling us to get up quickly and dress, as Indians were about. Such a scrambling for clothes in the dark. A light was not to be thought of. A regular mix-up of children and clothes occurred, which the mother alone could straighten out. The little folks seemed rather to enjoy the excitement. Several shots were exchanged, but the Indians, who were undoubtedly Crows on a horse stealing raid, soon as they found themselves discovered, disappeared. We retired again, but did not sleep much.

We drove to Bozeman next day. A few miles from the town we met seventy or eighty Crows, escorted by Lieutenant Doane, on their way to intercept the Nez Perce.[10] They looked rather more dangerous than any we had met. After reaching Bozeman, my brother eventually went with this party nearly to Mammoth Hot Springs in his endeavor to reach the point where

---

10 Gustavus Cheney Doan was a cavalry officer who accompanied the Washburn Expedition that explored the park in 1870 and led an army company attempting to contain the Nez Perce there in 1877 when the Indians fled their homeland in Idaho.

Mr. Cowan was shot but was compelled to return again to Bozeman without accomplishing that result.

In the meantime I had reached my father's home. Kind friends and neighbors had kept the news of our capture from my people until the day we reached home, then prepared them for our coming, thus sparing them much of the suspense. I reached there worn out with excitement and sorrow. Years seemed to have passed over my head since I had left my home a month previous.

From the time I learned of the close proximity of General Howard's command to the Nez Perce at the time Mr. Cowan was shot, I could not but entertain a faint hope that the soldiers might have found my husband alive. Yet, in reviewing all the circumstances, I could find little to base such a hope on. Still, as one after another of the party were accounted for, all living, the thought would come. I believed I should know to a certainty when my brother returned from his quest.

I had been home a week, when one afternoon two acquaintances drove to the house. My father not being in, I went to the door. They would not come in, but talked a few minutes on ordinary subjects. Then one of them handed me a paper and said news had been received of Mr. Cowan that he was alive.

In the *Independent* extra I found this account:

INDEPENDENT EXTRA

Cowan alive.

He is with General Howard's command.

Special to the Independent—Bozeman, September 5. Two scouts just in from Howard's command say that Cowan is with Howard and is doing well and will recover. He is shot through the thigh and in the side and wounded in the head. Howard was fourteen miles this side of Yellowstone Lake.

Some way the doorstep seemed conveniently near as a resting place just at that particular time. Presently they told me the particulars. He was badly wounded, but would live, was with Howard's command, and would either be sent back to Virginia City or brought the other way to Bozeman. For the time being, this news was all sufficient. A day or two passed. I learned nothing more. My brother Frank came but had the same news only that had been given me. The hours began to drag. I decided to go to Helena with my brother, as from that point telegraphic news could reach me much sooner. After arriving in Helena, however, a whole week passed before a telegram came to me, stating my husband would be in Bozeman the following day.

I lost no time going. At Bozeman, however, I found that he had given out at the Bottler ranch on the Yellowstone. A double-seated carriage was procured for the trip, and once again I found myself traversing the familiar and oft traveled road. But this day the sun shown. My husband had notice of my coming and was expecting me. I found him much better than I dared anticipate, and insistent on setting out for home without delay.[11]

We arranged robes and blankets in the bed of the carriage. With his back propped up against the back seat, he was made quite comfortable. We stopped for a handshake and congratulations at the Ferrill home on Trail Creek. We had a rather spirited team and made fair progress. Late in the afternoon we were at a point seven miles from Bozeman, in Rocky Canyon. The road was graded around a steep hillside for some distance. We could look down and see the tops of trees that grew on the stream far below. Presently we experienced the novel and very peculiar sensation of seeing our carriage resting on those same trees, wheels uppermost, and ourselves a huddled mass on the roadside. A broken pole strap caused the carriage to lunge forward of the horses as it ran up against them. The buggy tongue caught, snapped and threw the carriage completely over. Fortunately the seats were not fastened and we were left—a bundle of seats, robes, blankets and people on the hillside—shaken but not much hurt. The carriage, from which the horses had freed themselves, made one revolution as it went over and landed as described. We were thankful to have left it at the first tip.

Mr. Cowan was lifted to a more comfortable position by the roadside. Not long after, a horseman leading a pack animal came along. Our driver borrowed the horse, making the trip to Fort Ellis and back in the shortest possible time and returning with an ambulance. Seven miles seemed long ones, and before we reached Bozeman Mr. Cowan was almost exhausted, his wounds bleeding and needing attention. He was carried by careful hands

11 Emma rushed to be by her husband's side, making the 175-mile trip in 36 hours. Normally it would have taken four days.

to a room in the hotel as soon as the crowd had thinned out somewhat. Mr. Arnold arranged to dress the wounds, and in order to do so, seated himself on the side of the bed, when lo, the additional weight caused the whole inside of the bed to drop out and down on the floor. This sudden and unexpected fall, in his enfeebled state, nearly finished him. A collapse followed, from which he did not rally for some time.

A week passed before we were able to travel farther. By the time we reached home Mr. Cowan was able to hobble about on crutches. The winter passed, however, before he was entirely well. A severe gunshot wound through the hip, a bullet hole in the thigh, a ball flattened on the forehead, and the head badly cut with rock. Few, indeed, are the men who could have survived so severe an ordeal.

Many years have passed since the events herein narrated occurred, yet retrospection is all that is needed to bring them to mind clear and distinct as events of yesterday—many years, since which life has glided on and on, with scarce a ripple beyond the everyday sunshine and shadow that falls to the lot of each and all of God's people.

Caught in an October Snowstorm

Carrie Strahorn—1882

Carrie Strahorn was an adventurous woman who refused to stay at home when her husband Robert ("Pard" as she called him) went on scouting trips for the Union Pacific Railroad. The Strahorns got free train passes, but Pard's job was to look for places far from transcontinental tracks that the company could promote as destinations. That meant they had to travel long distances by stagecoach.

The Strahorns visited Yellowstone in 1880 when the park was beginning a great transformation from a roadless to a genteel resort. The first road across the park had just been completed although tall tree stumps still made it almost impossible to cross with a wagon. Also George Marshall had built a crude hotel at the Lower Geyser Basin, the first of many that soon would be spread across the park.

Carrie was satisfied with Marshall's hotel, which had canvass partitions between rooms, and she befriended Mrs. Marshall who became the first white woman to have a baby in the park. Other tourists didn't speak highly of either the hotel or the Marshalls.

In addition to the Marshalls, the Strahorns met Philetus Norris, Yellowstone Park's second superintendent. Norris had recently finished the first road across the park. The Strahorns started across the new road in a light spring wagon but abandoned that effort when they found it full of stumps and steep grades. They decided it was better to travel on horseback.

Nonetheless, Carrie's descriptions of her adventures in Yellowstone make excellent story. Here's an abridged version of "Early Days in Yellowstone," a chapter of her 1911 book, Fifteen Thousand Miles by Stage, *which was illustrated by the famous Western artist Charles M. Russell.*

* * * *

Early Yellowstone tourists were allowed to climb at will over the terraces at Mammoth Hot Springs.
NATIONAL PARK SERVICE.

In the fall of 1880 my husband, Pard, and I made our first trip into Yellowstone—that land without peer in the known world. The Utah and Northern Railroad had now reached Red Rock on the southern border of Montana, whence and rough stage road of about one hundred miles took us to Virginia City, the real starting point for the park and where arrangements were soon completed for entering the great geyserland.

The Marshall and Goff Stage Company sent the first public conveyance into the park, 120 miles distant, and we were to be the first passengers. Many Virginia City citizens begged us not to take the trip so late in the fall as early snowstorms were too hazardous and too severe to allow the trip to be made safely. The story was several times told of the party of a dozen or more who had been overtaken a year or two before and all had perished. But the plans had been carefully in progress for some weeks, and with the hour at hand for the trip we could not be persuaded to yield such a privilege; we would take our chances and trust in God and good horses. With the best of drivers in Mr. Marshall himself, and Pard and I as the only occasionally of the stage, at just daylight on the morning of October 1, 1880, we heard the wheels go round, and soon we were whirling along the beautiful Madison valley.

We had a sumptuous breakfast in the tidy log cabin of Gilman Sawtell, who was a Yellowstone Park guide. Then on to the top of Raynolds Pass from which point the "Three Tetons" rose before us in all their grandeur, their glistening pinnacles shone in the dying sunlight, while the first snows covered their rugged outline, and mellowed the jagged rocks of three of the mightiest peaks of the Rocky Mountains.

There were numberless herds of antelopes that eyed us curiously and galloped away; the streams were alive with mountain trout. Poor Pard was crazy for his rod and reel.

Soon the island dotted waters of Henry's Lake claimed all attention with its deeply indented shores, and mountain guardians 3,000 feet high. The deep green of the pine trees in contrast with the autumnal foliage lent a rare charm to the five miles of waterway. Every little depression leading to the quiet lake carried its silvery rivulet bordered with willows and the brown and yellow grass made a strong contrast to the flaming sumac. The autumn panorama was a marvel of brilliancy that any lover of nature would rejoice to see. Here we were at the fountainhead of the great Snake River, which we later followed a thousand miles south and west to the Columbia and the Pacific Ocean.

The stage drew up to quite a pretentious building on the lakeshore about half past eight in the evening. But enthusiasm weakened when a nearer view of the house revealed no doors or windows, but in their places strips of canvas flapping over the openings.

The ranch house belonged to the same historical Sawtell who had given us such a good breakfast, but during the late Indian troubles he had abandoned this house before it was finished, and had cached his doors and windows for fear the house would be burned. He intended to return there and open a public house if travel increased, but it was a most forbidding place at that time. Not expecting company, the stockman, sheepherder and two mail carriers who were camping in the house were somewhat surprised to see a woman emerge from the darkness into the glare of the candlelight.

The house was without furniture except a few cooking utensils, an old stove, a pine table, and some crude stools to sit on. Mr. Marshall made himself busy trying to get supper from supplies that had been brought from his house in the Lower Geyser Basin. He said he was awfully glad I could eat beans, but it was a case of mustard or beans, and the mustard was out, so there was not much choice.

After supper Pard and I gathered our blankets to go back to the stage to fix a place to sleep, but Mr. Marshall insisted there was a nice lot of hay upstairs where we could be more comfortable. He handed us a candle and directed us to a stairway. It was a rickety passage, with the wind howling through every aperture. Once upstairs the room to which we were sent seemed about forty feet square. The glimmering candle would light only a corner of the great black space, and a gust of wind would blow out the glim at intervals until the place seemed full of spooks and goblins.

Pard and I gazed at each other when we could, and when we couldn't, well, maybe I cried—I don't quite remember. He had persuaded me to buy a very heavy pair of shoes in Virginia City, because the ground was so hot in some sections of the park that thin soles were not at all safe to wear, and would soon be burned through. Then he had proceeded to hold them up to ridicule all day, and I had finally wagered five dollars with him that in spite of their looks I could get both of my feet into one of his shoes, if I was from Chicago. So there in the dim candle light, with any number of sashless and paneless windows, with the pallet of hay down in a dark corner, partly covered with canvas, with the wind shrieking requiems for the dead and threats for the living and with the rafters full of bats, I called to him to bring me his shoe, and let me win my wager.

I put on his number seven and declared my foot was lost and lonesome in it, and he cried out, "Well, then, now put in the other one! Put in the other one!" I began at once taking it off to put it on the other foot, when he cried out, "Oh, no, not that way, but both at once." But I revolted and said, "No, that was not in the bargain; I had not agreed to put both in at the same time." In deep chagrin he threw a five-dollar gold piece at me, which was lost for half an hour in the hay before I could find it, while he gave a grunt or two that will be better not translated. And so we went on with our merrymaking, trying to forget our surroundings, and dispel thoughts of our discomfort, but it was a glad hour that saw us started again on our way with a new sun.

We fared better for breakfast than we had for supper, although it was served on a bare table with tin dishes. One of the mail carriers came back to the house to tell me there was not another woman within thirty-five miles of

Henry's Lake. That reminded me of Col. Paul Vandervoort, an earlier writer on the marvelous charms of this section, who said that "lovely woman's sweet voice" had never floated across the surface of that placid lake, and we wondered whether the charm for him would now be broken because a woman's voice had floated thereon.

Henry's Lake is a magnificent duck-shooting resort, and with that and Goose Marsh so close together, where the mallards, redheads, teals, and canvas-backs flock by the million, there is joy unlimited for the hunter.

Leaving Henry's Lake our course was almost due east into the park; part of the drive was over a natural boulevard on a smooth plateau dotted with pines and elevated about thirty feet above the Madison River. At the end of this beautiful drive we reached the Riverside station, where one trail branched through the Madison Canyon, and the other climbed over hilltops to Lower Geyser Basin. The stage company had chosen the latter route and from the summit we obtained a glorious view of the valley and surrounding ranges of mountains. It was not until darkness settled around us that we reached the Lower Geyser Basin, at the entrance of which stood the new and unfinished little log house built by Mr. Marshall. It was with a twinge of disappointment that we were obliged to retire without seeing a geyser, but needing rest we were soon tucked away for the night and locked in slumber.

Next morning there was an early review of our surroundings; the log house was far from being finished, and the part we occupied was partitioned off with a canvas wagon cover. The second floor was only partly laid, and a window or two was missing in the upper part while the unfilled chinks between the logs allowed the rigorous October breezes to fan us. At that time the office and sitting room and dining room were one, and a single stove did its best toward heating the whole house. It was amid such cold discomfort during the season that followed that Mrs. Marshall gave birth to the first white child born in the park and the parents urgently requested me by letter to give the child a name. Mr. Marshall said the first white woman to completely tour the park should name the first white baby born there.[1]

In the frosty morning air the steam was rising from every point of vision and the whole ground seemed to be on fire, for boiling springs and geysers were almost without number. The first point to visit was the cluster of springs

---

1 Several other women had done complete circuits of the park earlier, but the Marshall's was the first white child born in the park.

two miles from the hotel. The road was through fine meadowland and groves, and beside a rippling stream that was fed only by the overflow of the springs in question.

The first one reached was known as the Thirty Minute Geyser as that is the interval of time between its eruptions. It was getting ready to spout when we arrived and gurgled and groaned and spouted a little; then after lying away to breather its force, it dashed up in the air some twenty feet and sustained its height for three minutes. There were other springs only a few feet away that constantly boiled but did not spout. A quarter of a mile from this cluster the Queen Laundry Geyser covered an area of at least an acre and a half. The main basin of the Laundry was not over fifty feet across, but it flowed down in a series of pools nearly half a mile from its source and there Became cool enough to bathe in, and to do Laundry work, for which its waters were especially adapted. Around the boiling basin were various formations of a brittle nature from a pure white to a dark crimson, giving the whole rim a brilliant rainbow brightness.

The boiling pots close by had overflowed until they built around themselves huge walls some thirty feet high. The center of the mound had an opening thirty feet in diameter and as round as a ring, with the water boiling and seething from a bottomless pit amid walls of fire.

These springs filled us with astonishment and were inclined to be angry when told that we must not loiter for they were scarcely worth the trouble to see when so much grander ones were but a few miles away. Near one of the small laundry geysers sat a workman who had been haying in a meadow close by and whose facial expression betokened deep trouble. After some questioning he said the boys told him that if he put his woolen shirt in the geyser when it was getting ready to spout that the cleansing waters would wash it perfectly clean while it whipped it in the air. He had followed their advice and was holding a piece of flannel about three inches square in his fingers he said that it was all he could find of his shirt when the waters got quiet, and he said he guessed it had gone down to H- to be ironed and he marched declaring he would "lick them fellers" if they not buy him a new shirt.

Leaving the Lower Basin, we followed up the east bank of the west fork of the Firehole River with geysers all along until we reached the big springs or geyser lakes, where we crossed the river and drove up to a level. The place was rightly named "Hell's Half Acre."[2] As I looked into the black depths,

2 Now called Midway Geyser Basin.

when the breeze blew the fumes from us, the groaning of the waters was heard like evil spirits in dispute. The surface of the Half Acre measured 250 feet in diameter.[3]

The spring had no period of eruption and it was not seen in its greatest glory until 1886 when visitors to the park who happened to be in the vicinity witnessed a rare spectacle. It was named the Excelsior Geyser because it is undoubtedly the most powerful geyser in the world. It suddenly broke out about three o'clock one Friday afternoon and continued to play twenty-four hours.

The witnesses pronounce it the grandest and most awe-inspiring display ever beheld. The spoutings were heard several miles distant, while the earth in the immediate vicinity was violently shaken as if by an earthquake. The noise of escaping steam, and the internal rumbling were deafening. An immense body of rumbling, deafening water, accompanied by steam, was projected to an altitude of about three hundred feet, and the Firehole River, which is only a few rods distant, soon became a torrent of boiling water. The display was kept up, with gradually decreasing force, until the Excelsior went back to its normal state.

Above the Half Acre we crossed back to the east side of the river and found a spring boiling up through an old hollow stump. It stood so close to the river that the waters washed it slightly on one side. The stump was three feet high, the water boiled constantly two feet above the top of it, directly through the heart of the stump, which was gradually becoming petrified.

Without waiting to examine the hundred or more geysers on our way, we continued up the river to the Riverside and Fan Geysers, where we again forded the stream and continued on until we reached the Castle Geyser, where we pitched our camp. The Castle seemed to be making a terrible fuss about something. Its crater looked more like a lighthouse than the ruins of a castle; it was indeed beautiful and majestic.

Above the Castle was Old Faithful, so called because of its perfect regularity, for every hour it throws the spectator into ecstasies of delight.[4] It is so

---

3 Hell's Half Acre was a popular name for what is now called the Midway Geyser Basin. Strayhorn apparently is describing the crater of the Excelsior Geyser, which was once the world's largest, throwing a curtain of water 300 feet wide up to 300 feet high in the decades around the dawn of the 20th century. Long dormant, it revived briefly in 1985 throwing water up 60 feet.

4 When they were first recorded, intervals between Old Faithful eruptions were about 65 minutes. The interval has lengthened across time and now is about 90 minutes but is variable.

regular in time of spouting that it has often been called the "Big Ben" of the park, after the famous old Westminster clock of London. One hundred and fifty feet it threw its column of water six feet in diameter, and held it unbroken sometimes for ten minutes, and never less than five minutes.

We returned to our horses and moved our camp for the night farther down the stream to a little point of timber between the Grotto and the Giant. Both of these latter named geysers showed signs of eruption, and while partaking of our supper the former seemed greatly agitated. We dipped the dishes in a hot spring close by and they were washed and wiped at the same time. The dome of the Grotto was remarkable. Over the center of the main opening an arch obstructed direct passage of the water. The force with which the water had been thrown back on the sides of the cave had worn great holes through the walls, forming a half dozen or more orifices through which water poured with great force.

We had no tents, and with only the stars for a canopy we lay in the midst of the greatest wonders of the world—with a roar like many storms

People used to be able to climb all over Yellowstone's geothermal features like these tourists are at Grotto Geyser.
NATIONAL PARK SERVICE.

and battalions of artillery breaking the quiet air. With the ground for a mattress and pine boughs for a pillow we passed the night in waiting, listening and sleeping, by turn, but withal we rested our tired limbs and made ready to endure the fatigues still ahead of us.

The morning after our return from the Upper Geyser Basin our party, including Mr. Marshall, Pard and myself, started for the Mammoth Hot Springs in a light wagon. It was necessary to make it a two-day trip because of the numerous points of interest along the way—and also because of the horrible road. There are no adjectives in our language that can properly define the public highway that was cut through heavy timber over rolling ground, with the stumps left from two to twenty inches above ground, and instead of grading around a hill it went straight to the top on one side and straight down on the other; whereas a few hundred dollars, properly expended, would have made it one of the finest drives in the world.

We had to abandon the light wagon and returned for a new start on horseback, for it was impossible to get any conveyance over the stumpy road.[5] It was the only attempt at a road in the park and what had been done with the government funds was pretty hard to see. The trails in the park, with one or two exceptions, were very difficult to follow and we often lost our way.

Soon we were trotting along to the Norris Plateau, or Norris Geyser Basin. This plateau embraced twenty-five square miles and seemed to be not only the most elevated and largest, but may also have been the most important and doubtless the oldest geyser basin in the park. It certainly was the hottest and most dangerous for pedestrians. The first little joker we reached was the Minute Geyser, and with an orifice of only a few inches it spurted up some five feet every sixty seconds, and then died down and showed not a ripple on its placid surface until it spurted again on time without any warning. To the right of the Minute Geyser was the Mammoth Geyser, and well it deserves its name. When it is quiet one can go up to the crater and study its beaded chimney, and look down its long dark throat, and shudder. Its chimney was about four feet high, with an orifice two feet by three feet in diameter. Its voluminous outbursts have fairly disemboweled the mountain at whose base it stands for a distance of a hundred feet or more, and at least

---

5 Two wagons had traversed the road earlier in 1880 according to W.W. Wylie who later established a system of permanent camps for Yellowstone tourists.

forty feet in width, while its greatest depth that can be seen does not exceed twenty feet.

A few miles beyond the Norris Basin was passed the base of Obsidian Mountain, which looms up like a sheet of glass. Its shiny surface gives many colors in sunlight, including black, brown, yellow, and red. Every little splinter has the same glassy appearance as the mass.

The Mammoth Hot Springs of the Gardner River were at last in sight, after a very long, hard pull over a mountain, where several times we felt riveted to the spot, unable to go another step from sheer exhaustion.

The gorge in which the Mammoth Springs are located is over 1,200 feet above the level of Gardner River. From the river up there are fourteen terraces, and the largest and hottest springs are near the top. The waters have rolled down and deposited their lime until they have built huge bowls or reservoirs one after another. The limestones, which dip under the river extend under the hot springs, and are doubtless the source of lime noticed in the waters and deposits on the terraces as they are secure and firm. There is so much lime that it gives the whole earth a white appearance, while the inside of these natural bathtubs seem to be porcelain lined and the water is a beautiful blue white. The outside crusting is rough and uneven with stalactites in profusion, which in some instances united with the stalagmites from the terrace below.

Each level or terrace has a large central spring, and the water bubbling over the delicately wrought rim of the basin flows the declivity, forming hundreds of basins from a few inches to six to seven feet in diameter and often seven feet in depth. The main terrace has a basin thirty by forty feet across, and the water is constantly boiling several inches above the surface: but a careful approach will permit one to peep into the reservoir and get a glimpse of the mossy vegetable matter that lines its sides in a rich light green that constantly waves with the ebullition of the water, and as the blue sky is reflected over all it lends an enchantment that no artist can duplicate.

Our attention was called to a monument some fifty feet high and twenty feet in diameter. No one was able to give any reason for its existence. The top was shaped like a cone and on the very summit was a funnel-shaped crater, which would lead one to believe that it had once been an active geyser, but it bore the significant title of "Liberty Cap."

On the terrace just above Liberty Cap is a fountain known as the "Devil's Thumb." I poked my head into one of the many large caverns which had once been boiling reservoirs, and inhaled the sickening fumes of Hades. I not only expected to see his Satanic Majesty's thumb, but his entire self as well, and could fancy he would drag me in and carry me down for his dinner.

The sky was full of threatening clouds the morning that our little party started out with saddle and pack animals for the upper Yellowstone River. We followed the same old Indian trail that General Howard and his troops did three years before,[6] and although there had not been a dollar spent on the road it was the only respectable trail in the whole park. For miles we rode along the cast fork of the Firehole River, and then began a slow but steady ascent of the Rockies' main

After starting on this climb we saw what seemed to be a flying centaur coming rapidly toward us, but it proved to be the wings of Colonel Norris' greatcoat flying in the wind as he rode madly down the trail. We had missed him at the Mammoth Springs, and now he insisted upon retracing his steps and making one of our party. He started ahead over a trail so plain that a child could not lose it—the only visible trail we had found. Every half mile he told to us to not worry about getting lost as he would keep in the lead and there was no danger. Colonel Norris was the superintendent of the park.

Darkness had settled when we reached the Yellowstone River and we hastened into camp. Pard had been commissioned to get an elk on a neighboring hill and Colonel Norris rode ahead to select the camp.[7] Mr. Marshall and I rode more until the colonel called us to the camp of his selection.

Instead of selecting a place under good trees, he had stopped in the middle of an opening on a side hill. The rain began to fall almost as soon as we were out of the saddles. Pard had come in without his elk, and betokened a dismal night. The beds were made at once and covered with canvas to keep them as dry as possible. I longed for something good to be brought out of the mess chest, but it was the same old bread and bacon, and the same old excuse from Mr. Marshall, but a ride of thirty-five miles made us glad to get even that.

---

6 General Oliver Otis Howard pursued the Nez Perce across the park in 1877 when the Indians fled their homeland to avoid being forced onto a reservation.

7 Hunting was allowed in Yellowstone Park from when it was established in 1872 until the army took over administration in 1886. Trophy and commercial hide hunters had been decimating park wildlife.

After supper we stood around the fire to dry our clothing, but as fast as one side was dry another side was wetter than ever, and thus we kept whirling around as if on a pivot until we gave up and went to bed, wet to the skin. We were lulled to sleep by the deep, sonorous voice of Colonel Norris who forgot to stop talking when he went to sleep and he was still talking right along when we woke up at midnight.

The rain changed to snow, and through the storm we saw the disconsolate face of Mr. Marshall, as he stood near the smoldering campfire muttering to himself as if he had become demented. Upon our inquiring the cause of his trouble, he said that as soon as he saw the snow he went to look for the horses—and they were gone.

"Gone!" we all exclaimed in unison and despair. The horses were gone and we were at the end of our rations with a big storm upon us. The many warnings not to go into the park so late went buzzing through our minds like bumblebees. The snow was several inches deep and falling faster every minute.

As soon as daylight came the men started in search of the horses. I was left all alone in the camp for several hours waiting with my rifle in hand, until after a hard and hurried chase the horses were overtaken and brought back. We knew that we should hurry home as quickly as possible—but to be within five miles and not to see the falls was asking too much. With the return of the horses we resolved at once to go on.

Superintendent Norris thought it was not best for me to go to the falls. The trip must be a hasty one, and the start home not to be delayed longer than possible for fear of continued storm. The snow ceased falling soon after daylight, but the sun did not appear and there was every indication of more snow. Pard was reluctant to leave me, and knew what disappointment lurked in my detention, but he was overruled. With Mr. Norris he started off leaving me with Mr. Marshall—who was to have everything ready for the return to Firehole Basin on their return.

The more I meditated the more I felt that I could not give up seeing the canyon and falls. To be balked by a paltry five or ten miles was more than I could stand. I called to Mr. Marshall to saddle my horse at once for I was going to the falls.

He laughingly said "all right," but he went right on with his work and made no move toward the horse. I had to repeat the request the third time most emphatically and added that I would start out on foot if he did not get my horse without more delay.

He said I could not follow them for I would not know the way, but I reminded him of the freshly fallen snow, and that I could easily follow the trail. He was vexed with my persistence as I was with his resistance, and he finally not only saddled my horse but his own, and rather sulkily remarked that if the bears carried off the whole outfit I would be to blame. When well on our way I persistently urged him to return to the camp and he finally did turn back, but waited and watched me until I turned out of sight.

Alone in the wild woods full of dangerous animals my blood began to cool, and I wondered what I should do if I met a big grizzly who would not give up the trail. The silence of that great forest was appalling and the newly fallen snow made cushions for the horse's feet as I sped noiselessly on. It was a gruesome hour, and to cheer myself I began to sing, and the echoing voice coming back from the treetops was mighty good company.

The five miles seemed to stretch out interminably. When about a mile from the falls other voices fell on my ear, and I drew rein to locate the sound, then gave a glad bound forward for it was Pard on his way back. Mr. Norris said anyone might think that Pard and I had been separated for a month, so glad were we to see each other.

Pard could not restrain his joy that I had followed, and sending the superintendent on to the camp he at once wheeled about and went with me to the falls and canyon that I came so near missing. Up and down o'er hills and vales we dashed as fast as our horses would carry us the upper falls were reached where we dismounted and went tip to the edge of the canyon to get a better view.

The upper falls are visible from many points along the canyon, and the trail runs close to them and also by the river for several miles, the tourist many glimpses of grandeur. Above the upper falls, the river is a series of sparkling cascades, when suddenly the stream narrows to thirty yards, and the booming cataract rushes over the steep ledge a hundred and twenty feet and rebounds in fleecy foam of great iridescence. The storm increased and the heavens grew darker every hour, but we pushed on.

Moran has been chided for his high coloring of this canyon, but one glimpse of its rare, rich hues would convince the most skeptical that exaggeration is impossible.[8] We longed to stay for days and weeks and hear this great anthem of nature and study its classical and noble accompaniment, but there was a stern decree that we must return, and that without delay.

There was no hope for sightseeing as we kept on our way back to the Lower Geyser Basin. Without giving our horses or ourselves over half an hour to rest at noon, we rode on and on, up hill and down, through woods and plains, until at last the lights of Marshall camp were in sight. The storm had continued all day, turning again from snow to rain in the valley. How tired I was when we rode up to the door. Our forty-mile ride was ended at seven o'clock, but it took three men to get me off my horse.

We left the park with the hope of spending a longer season there at an early day as there were many places of interest that we had to lightly pass and perhaps many that we did not see at all. There is not a section of the park that has not its peculiarities.

With beds on the hard ground and little over us but the stars, with modest fare to work on, and blind trails to follow, the trip through the park was in marked contrast to the elegant coaching trip of the present day, where boulevards lead the traveler to luxurious hotels at convenient intervals for his night of rest. But we had the compensation in the charms of nature which go with the wilderness and wonders in all their primal glory.

When full day came over the hills we cast a long admiring glance over the magnificent view and were borne reluctantly away to the Rodgers House in Virginia City. We roughly estimated that more than four hundred miles of travel in the park had been made on horseback.

It was with a twinge of disappointment that we were obliged to retire without seeing a geyser, but needing rest we were soon tucked away for the night and locked in slumber.

---

8 Landscape artist Thomas Moran accompanied the Hayden Expedition of 1871. His famous painting of the Yellowstone Canyon and Falls is credited with helping persuade the U.S. Congress to establish Yellowstone Park.

An "Old Lady"
Tours with Young People

HWS—1881

Little is known about the woman who wrote of the following piece for the Friends' Quarterly Examiner *on May 9, 1883. The magazine identifies the author only as HWS, and she reveals few details about herself, just that she was a stout lady 50 years old who had three children.*

We know that HWS was adventurous because she took her trip at a time when getting to Yellowstone Park required a long horseback or stagecoach ride. Road building was just beginning in Yellowstone Park so HWS knew she would have to ride a horse when she was there.

HWS describes preparations for her Yellowstone adventure and the trip from Ogden, Utah, to Camas, Idaho, on the Utah and Northern Railroad. In a few more years thousands would take the train all the way to Yellowstone Park and tour it in comfortable coaches. But in 1881, when HWS went there, it was still a remote wilderness with only a few primitive roads.

After reaching the end of the railroad line, HWS traveled with a pack train through scorching days and freezing nights across Idaho to the edge of Yellowstone National Park. She describes the wonders of geyserland and the joys of evenings around the campfire.

At the Lower Geyser Basin HWS abandoned her wagon and mounts "a sober old creature named Foxey" to cross the roadless wilderness to the Grand Canyon of the Yellowstone. She then visited Yellowstone Lake and the Upper Geyser Basin. Then she starts home.

* * * *

In the summer of 1880, while traveling in California, we conceived the idea of taking a trip the following year to the National Yellowstone Park. This celebrated region is 55 miles by 60 in extent, and in 1872 was set apart by

Congress as a "National Park" forever. It is beyond Salt Lake, and is, roughly speaking, from 33 to 34 west longitude from Washington, and from 44 to 45 north longitude.

Our party consisted of myself and three children, two young collegians, two gentlemen from Philadelphia, and a young cousin. As we had learned that our journey would have to be largely made on horseback, we condensed our baggage as much as possible, and packed it in some admirable canvas saddlebags we found in an outlying store at Salt Lake. Our "proud clothes" we left in Ogden to be picked up on our return.

During our previous camping-out trip in Colorado, we had discovered that an oval hole dug for the hips relieved the strain on the body, and made even the hard earth quite bearable. And if to this was added a small pillow to place under the back or side, it became luxurious! We therefore purchased pillows at Salt Lake, and I supplied myself with a private trowel to carry in my own knapsack for these digging purposes. The three ladies of the party (myself and my two daughters) wore short flannel suits, with Turkish trousers. The gentlemen wore flannel shirts, and winter coats and pants, with brown duck overalls for protection from rents and holes. These latter garments were bought at my especial request, as I strongly objected to the risk of spending all my spare time in mending.

On July 27th we started for Camas on the little narrow gauge railroad, our road lying through the dreariest of all dreary alkali plains. As far as the eye could reach, there was nothing to be seen but the burning and the sad gray sagebrush, which is the only thing that will grow upon it. Prairie the people called it, but desert it is, and desert it used to be called, I am sure, in the geographies of my childhood. I remember well how I used to be interested and excited in those far off days with the vague descriptions given us of this mysterious "Great American Desert," and how used to long to penetrate its dreary wastes, but never hoped to have such good fortune bestowed upon me.

And now here I found myself, feeling as natural and almost as much at home as on a New Jersey sand-flat, and could hardly wonder how it came about. I believe it is the tin cans that have done it—tin cans and Yankee push and grit, but chiefly tin cans, for without them I do not see how these deserts could have been traversed or settled. The altitudes are so high, and the nights so cold, and the water so scarce, that nothing fit to eat grows naturally, and

Many tourists like these women decided to provide their own tents and transportation rather than pay to stay in hotels or commercial camps.
GALLATIN HISTORY MUSEUM.

very little can be raised artificially, and therefore if it had not been for the ease of carrying food in these cans, civilization would, it seems to me, have met with an impassible barrier in these desert plains.

We were met on the little railroad platform at Camas by our guides, three fine looking mountaineers, who informed us that they had a train of twenty-six horses and mules ready for our trip. We had also engaged a Chinese cook at Ogden, named Tin Lee, a very obliging fellow, and excellent in his profession.

So far things looked promising, but it was perfectly hot, and the wind blew almost a hurricane all the time, and the sand was whirled in through every crack in such quantities as absolutely to necessitate closed doors and windows, and all day long it was simply unmitigated discomfort. They told us it had only rained twice there in four years, and we could almost believe it, though we could not but suspect that this was one of the stories told to "tender feet," as all new comers in the West are called.

51

We wore through the day, somehow, however, and at night were repaid for all our troubles. The storekeeper allowed us to spread our bedding in his hay-yard the air cooled off rapidly with the going down of the sun, and with the sweet, soft hay beneath us, and the glorious clear sky above us, we felt we had beds that a monarch might envy. No physical sensation in the world appears to me to be more delightful than that of sleeping in the open air on a clear, cool night, with plenty of blankets and buffalo robes around and underneath one.

To have all the wide universe to breathe into, and the infinite sky to gaze upon, seems to lift one out of this ordinary everyday world into a region of glorious possibilities and undreamed of triumphs. Next morning the guides brought the riding horses up to the store, and we all went out and tried them, in order to find out those which would best suit our individual likings. This was fun to the young people, but I am free to confess it was misery to me, for I had not been on the back of a horse for years, and had long ago decided that, being in my fiftieth year, and rather stout, my time for horseback riding was over. I tried several, but found them all so slippery that I experienced a great tendency to fall off their backs the moment they undertook to go out of a walk, especially as we had to use Spanish saddles, with only a high peak in front. The prospect began to look very dreary to me, as the guides said we should have five or six hundred miles to travel in this way.

I began to ask myself if even the "Mystic Wonderland" would pay for such a journey. But of course, the party could not be stopped by any whim of mine, so I made up my mind to say nothing, and just "grin and bear it." However, at last we found a light two-seated wagon in the town, which we bought with the hope of selling it again on our return, and two of our pack-mules were found to pull it, so that this difficulty was surmounted for the time, though our guides seemed to think it very doubtful whether a wagon would be able to travel over the rough trails into the park.

We made an imposing appearance as we started off with our long train of three guides, ten packhorses, nine horseback riders, the wagon with its occupants, two dogs, and three little colts, who were accompanying their mothers on the trip. The next morning, however, we were greeted with the intelligence that our horses and mules had strayed away during the night and were lost! The search for them occupied several hours, and after we had resumed our journey, the wagon made our route much more perplexing on account of the difficulty of fording the streams.

The sun seemed to scorch like a fire, and the wind, which might have been a comfort had it been moderate, seemed to take away our breath by its fierceness. We wondered if there was any comfort possible in a country that is both hot and windy at once. No one can have an idea of these winds who has not felt them. They seem to blow you back in your life somehow, and you have to use all your energies to catch up again. Our night experiences were peculiar. We had to go to bed and get up in the midst of a vast airy space, with no shelter for anything. Of course no one thought of undressing much, but the little we did need to do for comfort's sake was an affair of highest art, as may readily be imagined.

Though the days were so sultry, the nights were bitterly cold, and it was quite a common thing for us to find ice half an inch or an inch thick in our basins or buckets when we woke in the morning; and this in August! This extreme change of temperature is caused by the excessively dry air, which does not retain heat like a moist atmosphere; in consequence of which it cools off the moment the sun's rays leave it. The lower layers of atmosphere, rarefied with the day's heat, all rise, and the cold winds from the mountains rush in to fill their place. For two days, we had not seen a single human being, and not even a dog, or horse or cow. On the third day, however, to our delight, we met a man and his wife, traveling with all their household goods from Montana to Ogden, and they gave us some information about the route.

We camped that night in a beautiful green meadow, and though we tried to toast our poor cold feet at our fire before going to bed, we arose in the morning shivering with cold, Mr. S having dreamed that he was asleep in an icehouse, and all the rest of us having had equally delightful sensations. Our slumbers were also disturbed by a stampede of our horses, which were frightened by a flock of wild swans, and came tearing and racing almost over our very beds, but were fortunately turned off in another direction by two of our young men jumping out at them, and they were finally quieted by our guides.

On the third of August we entered the park. The first point we reached is what is called the Firehole, or the Lower Geyser Basin. It is a flat meadow, 7,000 feet above the sea, through which runs the Firehole River, and part of it is covered with beautiful grass, while part of it is the white sinter formation of the hot springs and geysers. Setting Tin Lee to work at his stove preparing supper, we rode about a mile on the edge of the pine forest that skirted the weird, desolate plain of the geyser basin. It was one glare of white geyserite, with sulphur and iron and alum springs bubbling up all over it, and little steaming funnels everywhere, giving evidence of the internal fires beneath. Standing or lying about this plain are trees killed by the hot, siliceous waters. Nothing in nature could be more spectral than these naked trunks of trees, stripped of bark and bare of branches, and bleached white as snow, looking like the ghosts of the groves and forests, which are undoubtedly buried beneath the constantly accumulating mass of deposit.

It was a scene of absolutely uncanny desolation, and as we looked at it we ceased to wonder at the names bestowed upon it by its first discoverers, such as "Devil's Paint Pots," "Hell's Half-acre," etc.

One of our guides told us in graphic language of his first sight of this region. "You see," he said, "a party of us were out prospecting for mines, and we had traveled all day through pretty thick forests, and were pushing towards an opening we could dimly see through the trees, where, we hoped to make a comfortable camp for the night. We were very tired, and were hurrying to get into camp, when suddenly, just as we reached the edge of the forest without a moment's warning, we heard a most awful rumbling, the ground shook under our feet, and there burst into the air a column of water and steam that looked as if it reached the skies. We just fairly lost our senses, and never stopped to take a second look, but wheeled about in an instant, put spurs to our horses, and crushed away through the underbrush and tree-trunks as if the Evil One himself were after us. And the fact is," he added, "we did not know but that he was. For what else, we asked ourselves, could such goings-on mean, but that we were on the very edge of the lower regions? We never rested till we had put miles between us and that awful place, and for years we never spoke of it for fear the fellows should think we had really been to hell, and were sold to the old fellow who lives there."[1]

We could not wonder at the fright of men who had probably never heard of geysers or volcanoes, and who had no more expectation of coming across such phenomena in that quiet and lonely region than we in Philadelphia have of seeing them in our sober Fairmount Park.

---

1 Probably this story was made up to entertain the travelers, which was a common practice at the time. Travelers generally see signs of geothermal activity long before they see a geyser erupt, making unlikely that such events take them by surprise.

This is considered to be the most wonderful geyser region in the whole world. The far-famed geysers of Iceland are tame fountains compared to some here. It is estimated by Professor Hayden[2] that within an area of thirty-five or forty square miles there are at least 2,000 hot springs, steam-jets, geysers, and mud fountains; and in the whole park there are supposed to be not less than 10,000. Many of the geysers spout to the height of fifty or a hundred feet, some two or three hundred, and our guides even told us of one which has only been known to spout twice, but which, when it does perform, reaches, they declared, the stupendous height of seven hundred feet. But as we did not see this one, we felt a little dubious.

The geysers seem to have all sorts of openings. Some of them have formed craters around their mouths twenty or thirty feet high, that have assumed curious fantastic shapes and are constantly sending out between their eruptions great puffs of steam, and little jets of scalding spray, while there is all the time a sound of fierce boiling water below. In others the hot water stands, a marvelously transparent pool, in saucer-shaped basins, from ten to one hundred feet across, at the bottom of which is the well or tube from which the eruption issues. No language can adequately describe the gracefully curved and scalloped forms of the deposits which line the apparently bottomless sides of these openings, nor the countless vivid and delicate colors with which they are dyed, shading from a deep crimson, on the edge of the pool, to a glorious emerald green or sapphire blue in the center. To look down into the pure depths of these wonderful basins, with their fantastic forms and exquisite colors, is like looking into fairyland. Then suddenly, without a moment's warning, or any apparent cause, the quiet water will begin to heave, and boil, and spurt, and will dash into a marvelous cataract, apparently instinct with life; leaping towards the skies, just as a cataract leaps downward; breaking into rockets of milk-white spray, each of which sends out a burst of steam, and then falls to the white rocks below in showers of shining jewels, tinted with all the colors of the rainbow. A geyser eruption is not in the least like an artificial fountain, but more like an inverted cataract, filled with a mighty life, every instant changing its shape and its height, and is always enveloped and surmounted by vast clouds and pillars of steam that sway with the wind, the whole being crowned and tinged with rainbows.

---

2 Ferdinand Vandiveer Hayden was the leader of the first government expedition to explore the park in 1871.

These marvelous displays take place with one or two geysers at regular intervals, but most of them are very irregular in their times of action, varying from three or four hours to several days, or even two or three weeks. They seem sometimes to die out altogether, and new ones to break out in fresh places. It would seem, therefore, that while the amount of geyser action continues about the same, its centers of activity are constantly changing.

We were now a party of eleven, three sober middle-aged grown-ups, and eight young people, full of life and energy, and ready for any fun or adventure that came in their way. Our campfires at night were scenes of great merriment. As soon as we would get into camp all but the lazy ones would go to work gathering sagebrush or wood for the fire. We would choose a spot with dry sand or grass, and piling up our fuel and lighting it, would all gather round it on our rugs and buffalo robes, and tell stories and sing songs until bedtime. Tin Lee, our Chinese cook, was a great feature in these entertainments. He seemed such an innocent, guileless sort of creature, that one's heart was quite attracted to him, although all of us believed it was only the innocence and guilelessness of deepest cunning.

He would come up to the fire with a smile that was almost as childlike and bland as that of the immortal "Ah Sin," and take his place among us as innocently as though he belonged to us, and had a right to share all our pleasures. Sometimes we would get him to sing us a Chinese song—he called it "songing a sing"—and a sadder, more pathetic tune I never heard anywhere. It was always the same, and had no variations, and it seemed to embody in its sad refrain all the grief of a hopeless helpless race. It almost brought tears to my eyes every time I heard it. But I fear that our young people felt none of this, for they had persuaded the unsuspecting Tin Lee that he had a very fine tenor voice, and they would go into uncontrollable fits of laughter over the high falsetto quavers produced. These nightly campfires are the chief delight of the trip. The air is always cool enough to make the warmth agreeable, and the deliciousness of lying stretched out on one's buffalo robes under the open sky, around a high roaring fire, can only be understood by experience. It seems, too, as if every one's wits were sharper than usual under such circumstances, and our young party had many a grand night of it, that gave the three quiet elders almost as much delight as themselves. The only drawback would be the inevitable coming of ten o'clock, when the sound of my "Now, daughters, it is bedtime," was almost as dreaded as the cry of the panther would have been. There was only one other sound that spread greater consternation, and that was the call of Tin Lee in the morning when breakfast was ready. He would wake us up from our delicious naps by playing a tattoo on a tin pan, and calling out to us at the top of his funny, squeaky voice, "Hi there! Bleakfast! Flappee Jack! Flappee Jack! Him all done!"

Our route lay for two days through the parks of the Rocky Mountains. These are so wonderfully beautiful that I feel as if I wanted to make everybody see them.

Imagine an English nobleman's country seat set right down in the midst of these mountains, with great stretches of greenest grass, groups of beautiful trees, beds of brightest flowers, a winding, dashing mountain river, tiny lakes, slopes of turf, fantastic rocks scattered in the most romantic confusion, and around it all a girdle of grandest mountains, often flecked with snow, and changing continually from sunshine to storm, one hour covered with clouds, and the next standing out in clear cut beauty and sublimity against the deep blue sky. I confess that it stands out in my memory as the emblem of all that this world can give of peace and beauty and perfect rest; and to remember that these rugged mountains are full of such quiet nooks gives one a blessed sense of the sweetness of God's almighty power, which has delighted itself in such lovely bits of creation. We traveled over a road made of obsidian, which is a sort of volcanic glass, of a reddish black color, and glistened beautifully in the sun. We picked up some specimens, and found it was very much like the lumps that are thrown out of the melting pot in a glass factory when a pot breaks. It is very evident that the whole mountain was at one time a molten mass.

It is one of the boasts of the Yellowstone Park that it possesses the only glass mountain and glass road in the world. The road was made by building great fires on the glass mountain, upon which, after a thorough heating, cold water was dashed, thus cracking off large masses of glass, which were afterwards broken into small fragments with small picks and sledges. But I confess that I walked along that wonderful road, and looked up at that cliff in a very commonplace frame of mind. For the fact was I had been so unmercifully jolted over the stumps of trees and small rocks of which our "excellent carriage road" was composed that every bit of sentiment except fatigue had been shaken out of me, and I could not help thinking as much of the jolts that had been and the jolts that were to be as of the obsidian mountain.

At one of the hot springs along the bed of which we passed, some of our young people barely escaped a serious accident. They had dismounted, and gone down to get a drink at the river, when they saw a hot spring bubbling up in the edge of it, and crowded round it to see the curious phenomenon of a hot spring in a cold river. A crust of geyserite had been formed on the bank, and they rashly ventured upon it, when, to their dismay, it crashed through, and let them all down into the water! Fortunately, it was neither very deep nor very hot, as it was tempered by the cool water of the river, and no harm came of it but a temporary wetting.

When we reached the celebrated Mammoth Hot Springs, we felt that we were fully repaid for all our journey. The first impression on beholding it is that of a snow mountain, beautifully terraced into exquisitely shaped and colored basins, and with frozen cascades projecting on each side. At the top of this snowy hill, there is a large lake of boiling springs, which is exquisite in coloring, and full of most beautiful formations. It shades off from a deep crimson rim to a snowy white, and then to a deep emerald center, and seems to be filled with bunches of the finest spun glass, and with thousands of sinter ferns and mushrooms, and stalactites and flowers of all shapes and colors.

From this lake the water falls gently and quietly down the hill, dropping as it goes into a series of terraced basins, from a few inches to six or eight feet in diameter, and from one inch to several feet in depth. The margins of these basins were exquisitely fluted and scalloped, with a finish resembling the finest beadwork. Some were a delicate pink, some a lovely lemon, then an ultramarine blue, dark red emerald green, bright yellow, or a rich salmon; each basin perfectly distinct in form and color. The whole formed a scene that baffles description. When we reached the summit it was just sunset and the evening glow was over it all. The quiet water of the hot lake was rendered lovelier still by the sunset clouds that were reflected in its depths, and far off in the horizon lofty snowy mountain ranges bounded the view, with green valleys and dark canyons making rifts in their rugged sides—it was a dream of beauty! But there is no escaping the stern realities of life, and a camping-out tour has its drawbacks to the unmitigated enjoyment of the female head of the company, who feels the responsibility of having things moderately respectable.

As it may interest any other old lady who thinks of making such a trip, with a party of young people, to know what lies before her, I will describe my various grapples each day, beginning with the morning. We slept mostly, as I have said, right flat out in the middle of the plain, with generally not even a shrub to creep behind, and as we all kept near together for protection, it became a matter requiring no small skill to manage our times for getting up and going to bed satisfactorily, so as to create privacy where there was no material for it. Then came breakfast. Tin Lee made delicious "flappee jacks," as he called them, and all the young folks were "devoted" to them. And to keep account of whose turn it was to have one, and of the amount of honey, jam, or molasses that could be allowed to each, was a wonderful grapple. Next came the packing up for our start. First, the bedding of each one had to be rolled up into as complete a bundle as possible, and securely strapped, for the horses' backs; and to collect all the multitudinous wrappings, and superintend the rolling them up, required more vigilance and energy than anyone could think who has not tried it. Then the young people had to be marshaled, and their shawls and overcoats and waterproofs tied on to the backs of their saddles, and all the contingencies of weather—hot and cold, wet and dry—to be provided for; for after our pack train, with our baggage, once started in the morning, we never saw it again till we went into camp at night. Then the lunch for our whole party had to be provided and packed; and afterwards followed the grapples of the day's journey, the finding the trail, and the grappling with the rocks and roots and stumps and swamps over which it generally pursued its course; the fording of streams, the climbing of mountains, the crossing of gullies, the going down the steepest of hill sides, all in a continuous succession, one after another.

And to make matters worse for those of us who occupied the wagon, the trails often led along the sides of hills, and being simply "natural roads," i.e., not graded in the least, they, of course, slanted sideways, and kept us continually jumping from one side of the wagon to the other to make it balance, and keep it from toppling over.

Then, as noon drew near, and cries for lunch began to come from our hungry equestrians, there was the necessity of finding out a pleasant lunching place, where shade and water could be secured. After this would come the grapples of the afternoon journey and as evening drew on there would be the search for a good camping place, combining grass for our horses, wood for our fires, and water to drink for both man and beast. And lastly came the grapple for our night arrangements. A soft spot would have to be found for our sleeping, sheltered from the wind if possible, and then I would dig the small holes I spoke of, which so largely added to our comfort. All this had to be done, regardless of the holes and humps of all sorts and sizes, evidently the homes of wild creatures of various kinds, on the top of which our beds had to be spread. It was often a matter of speculation with me, when we lay down at ten o'clock, as to how we should grapple with any of these wild creatures, if they should take a notion to try and get out of their holes during the night. But I am thankful to say that, discouraged no doubt by our superincumbent weight, none of them ever did so. Finally, all the merry singing party had to be coaxed, or scolded, or inveigled into bed, which was no small grapple, as any mother will know. Besides all this, there was our "wash" to be attended to, for, be as economical as we would, still handkerchiefs and towels would get soiled, and even camping out did not render us entirely indifferent to cleanliness. I, as the oldest member of the party, had to keep up a continual grapple with wet feet, cuts, bruises, sunburn, etc., until sometimes I felt as if life was all one long grapple. Reading or meditating is pretty much out of the question in a trip like this, and for this reason it is an invaluable remedy for over-tasked brains and nerves. I felt as if we were all a party of cabbage-heads struggling for existence under most unfavorable circumstances.

The day we left the Mammoth Hot Springs, we had an accumulation of all the miseries of camping-out life. Fierce heat succeeded by torrents of wind and rain, and, to add to everything else, perfect swarms of mosquitoes. But we were repaid by the sight of Tower Creek, which rises in the high divide between the valleys of the Missouri and Yellowstone, and flows for ten miles through a cavern so deep and gloomy that it is called the Devil's Gorge. About two hundred yards before entering the Yellowstone River, it dashes over an abrupt descent of 156 feet, forming a very beautiful waterfall. All around are columns of volcanic breccia, some resembling towers, some the spires of churches, and some are almost as slender and graceful as the minarets of a mosque.

But, alas, one sad fatality spoiled the scene for me. It was impossible to take the wagon any further, and there was no alternative but to mount one of those wild beasts named by Adam a horse. The guides picked me out a sober old creature named Foxey, used to carry a pack, and likely therefore to be equal to my weight, and unlikely to be frisky or foolish. On the morning of the ninth of August, we started a long train of twenty-six horses, two

60

dogs, and three colts, for the Yellowstone Falls and Canyon. As I was quite determined never to go out of a walk, on account of the tendency to slip off, I took the tail end of the pack train, and plodded on very contentedly for a while. But, alas, my comfort was of short duration, for, when we stopped to lunch, Foxey lost sight of the pack, to which he felt he rightfully belonged, and getting either bewildered or angry, he began to behave in the most unaccountable manner. He backed and forwarded and sidled and turned round and round and neighed, and completely mastered me, till one of the guides came up and fastened a rope to his bridle and led him the rest of the way. It is beyond my power to depict the grandeur and beauty of the mystic river, and its falls and canyon. There are two falls, half a mile apart; the upper is 109 feet high, and the lower 308. The water is compressed into a mass about 100 feet wide, and from four to six feet deep, and falls over the precipices in one apparently solid mass of glorious emerald, into its marvelous canyon below. This canyon is one of the park's greatest wonders. It is a stupendous chasm about twenty-five miles long and from 1,000 to 3,000 feet high. It can only be seen from the top, as its sides are inaccessible except in one place six miles below the falls. The river has cut its way through a material largely composed of soft clays, sand, tufa, volcanic ash and breccia, with occasional layers of basalt, and has wrought out for itself a wonderful channel. Towers and turrets and dykes and castle walls of all shapes and sizes are crowded together throughout its whole length in wild confusion. Here and there a single tower stands out in solitary grandeur, isolated from all its fellows, with perhaps a lonely fish hawk's nest on its top, and little birds stretching out their open mouths towards the mother, who was circling in the grand and awful chasm over the river. But wonderful as these walls are for their height, and the grotesque and beautiful forms into which they are eroded, they are vastly more so for their color. From their lofty tops to the very edge of the water, they are dyed with an endless variety of the most vivid and delicate coloring. They are a mass of yellows and red and coal black and snow-white and cream and buff and brown and gray and olive, mingled together in richest confusion, while at the bottom runs the river, a glorious roaring torrent of purest emerald green, embroidered with silvery foam, between slopes decorated with velvet grass. The effect is indescribable.

The lads of our party found great delight in starting enormous fallen trees down the awful incline, and watching them crash their way with a fearful swiftness to the river's brink. Any mother will know how that made me feel, especially when I add that no doctor could be procured in that region under seven days at the very least, and that we had neither houses nor beds, nor anything considered necessary in sickness. I confess I was thankful every minute that our family did not possess a country seat on the banks of the Yellowstone Canyon!

Near us was camped a photographer, and of course we were taken, guides, pack train, colts, dogs and all. They put me, mounted on Foxey, in the very forefront of the picture, and beside me an old blind pack-horse with our store on his back, choosing this position for us, no doubt, because we were the two queerest looking objects in the whole train. We have since heard that this picture is to be put in a panorama amongst other objects of interest in the park, and that we shall be magnified to the size of fifteen feet and perfectly recognizable!

One of our chief difficulties arose from the impurity of the water and its impregnation with mineral substances, yet the whole of our party went through the trip without suffering any bad effects, and even grew stronger and better, though not a drop of any stimulant was touched by any of us.

The Yellowstone Lake lies 7,780 feet above the sea, almost on the top of the Rocky Mountains, and covers 300 square miles, being the fourth in size, which lies entirely within the limits of the United States. Its pure, cold waters, in some places 300 feet deep, are the rich blue color of the open sea, and swarm with trout, while it is the summer home of white swan, pelicans, geese, snipe, ducks, cranes, etc., and its shores furnish feeding grounds for elk, antelope, black and white tailed deer, bears, and mountain sheep.

Scattered along its shores are many clusters of hot springs and small geysers. It is surrounded on every side but one with snowy mountains, and was long considered to be entirely mountain-locked and inaccessible. The guides told us that it was literally true that a man could stand at one point on the shore of the lake and catch fish on one side of him, which he could swing over and cook in a boiling spring on the other side!

Leaving these high elevations, we went to see the Upper and Lower Geyser Basins. We had dismounted and unloaded our horses and buggy, and were looking for the best sites for our tents, when the cry was heard, "There goes a geyser!" and we dropped everything and ran. The sight was truly a glorious one. At the far end of the basin, Old Faithful was playing his wonderful fountain, and we saw what looked to us a river of water shooting up into the sky. Our guides told us it was only 150 or 200 feet high, but to us it seemed to reach the clouds, and on one side of it was a lovely soft rainbow that came and went with the blowing spray. It spouted for five or ten minutes and then subsided. Old Faithful is the only geyser whose performances can be depended upon. He spouts regularly every sixty-seven minutes, and has done so ever since the discovery of the park.[3] The crater looks like a great mound of coral or petrified sponge, surrounded by terraced basins at all shapes and sizes, and of the most lovely colors. The whole mound is convoluted in the most beautiful fashion, and every one of the little basins around it is rimmed with exquisite scalloping and fluting. The Grand Geyser, the Giant, the Grotto, the Splendid, the Riverside, and the Fan, complete the list of large geysers in this basin, and each one has a marvelous and distinct beauty.

As we were quietly sitting in camp the day after our arrival, I noticed a great steam in the direction of the Grand Geyser, and called out to one of our guides, "George, is old Grand doing anything?" He looked a moment, and then, dropping everything, began to run, shouting out at the top of his voice, "Old Grand is spouting! Old Grand is spouting!" In a second of time our camp was deserted, everything was left in wild confusion, and we were all running at the top of our speed to see the display. It was perfectly glorious! As it sent up its grand water rockets 250 feet into the air, shooting out on every side, we all involuntarily shouted and clapped our hands, and Sam took off his hat and swung it over his head in a perfect enthusiasm of delight! It was like a grand oration, and a wonderful poem, and a beautiful picture, and a marvelous statue, and a splendid display of fireworks, and everything else grand and lovely combined in one. Then all would subside, and the pool would be quiet for a moment or two; then again, it would heave and swell, and the glorious fountain would suddenly burst up again into the blue sky! Seven times this took place, and then all the water was sucked down, down, down into the abyss, and we climbed part way into the steaming crater, and picked up specimens from the very spot where just before had been this mighty fountain. The Giant, too, gave us a grand performance while we were in the Basin. We thought it the grandest and most beautiful of all. It shoots up a column of water at least seven feet thick to the height of 250 feet, the

---

3 The interval between Old Faithful's eruptions has lengthened across time. It is now about 95 minutes.

steam rising far higher. It played for nearly an hour, and flooded the whole basin around with boiling water, doubling the volume of water in the river. The internal rumblings and roarings meanwhile were perfectly deafening. I could not help feeling as I gazed on these wonders that there was a lesson in it all. Nothing but heat could bring forth such beauty as we see here at every step, and I thought that thus also did the refining fire of God bring forth in our characters forms and colors as beautiful after their fashion as these.

On the 19th, we broke camp and started for our homeward journey. And so, in due time, our trip was over, and the "Mystic Wonderland" lay behind us; but we all felt that we had stored up while there a treasure of fascinating memories of which no time nor distance could rob us. Some of us felt also that we had learned to know our God and His greatness as we had not known Him before, while living amid such displays of His creating and sustaining power, and realized that never again could we doubt His love and care.

Accommodations Were
Ludicrously Insufficient

Margaret Cruikshank—1883

In 1883 the Northern Pacific finished building its transcontinental railroad and opened Yellowstone Park to a flood of middle-class tourists from all over America. One of them was 58-year-old Margaret Andrews Cruikshank who took the newly completed Northern Pacific Railroad from her home in Minneapolis to Livingston, Montana. She then headed to the park via the spur line that ended then near the town of Corwin Springs. Workers finished the track all the way to the Gardiner on the park's northern border just twelve days later. A coach delivered her to the National Hotel at Mammoth Hot Spring. Although the National was still under construction and accommodations were unfinished, Margaret reserved her sharpest criticism for Marshall's Hotel at the Lower Geyser Basin.

Unfortunately for Margaret, she arrived in August when three VIP parties— one led by U.S. President Chester A. Arthur and another by Northern Pacific President Henry Villard, and a third by Rufus Hatch of the Yellowstone Development Company—were visiting the park. These dignitaries pre-empted hotel accommodations. Margaret and the few other unaccompanied women were left to fend for themselves—and seek help from Victorian gentlemen.

Margaret enjoyed the natural wonders, but was quick to condemn the tent hotels and crude log structures where she thought her hosts were serving horsemeat. Her diary is in the Yellowstone Park Library. An abridged version was published in Montana, The Magazine of Western History, *in 1960. The version here is abridged further.*

* * * *

The morning of August 23rd we left the Mammoth Hot Springs to make the round of the park. Our outfit was a light, strongly made two-seated vehicle, with an outside seat for the driver. It had a top and curtains all around that were kept rolled up for air and view. This vehicle was drawn by two strong horses, mountain-born and mountain-bred; for no other horseflesh could endure such toil for a day. Behind the carriage was a boot where were stored a small tent, blankets, and cooking utensils; oats and a bucket for the horses' use were not forgotten; while inside, under the seats, were boxes and baskets carrying provisions. Our wraps, waterproofs, handbags, and guidebooks also found places, and we were ready to start—four of us plus the driver.

What I have said about the horses will be appreciated when I state that the first thing was to climb Terrace Mountain. Within the distance of two miles, four "hitches" as they call them, carried us nearly 3,000 feet higher than the level of the hotel from which we started. At the steepest places we got out and walked—and then began our sufferings. The dirt was almost ankle deep and the heat and clarity of the air made it a serious business. Still it had to be done, if we expected those same horses to last through our journey. This may be laid down as certain: wherever you go there are streams to ford, corduroy to fall over, sagebrush plains to crawl along and mountains to cross. The strong can stand it, and enjoy it; but this is no place for the delicate. Even the strong would be satisfied with less of it. I never longed for railroads as I did there.

As we made our way to Norris, the first wonder was the Obsidian Cliffs, upheaved somewhat columnar masses of black volcanic glass suggesting mines of the finest anthracite. The road beneath them is macadamized with the fragments, a glass road a quarter of a mile long.

We had left the Hot Springs Hotel before eleven, and it was after dark when we reached Norris, so long are twenty-one miles in the park. It had been hot during the day, but as evening approached we were glad to draw about us heavy wraps. This was our constant experience. It was well that accident had prevented our wearing the usually advertised winter clothing; in the middle of the day especially when climbing hills, it would have been intolerable. Our faithful driver Isaac sometimes tried our patience by care for his horses, but we were satisfied afterwards that he was right, at the least we fared better than most.

As we started just in advance of the first detachment of the Hatch Party (some twenty-five—all that the slender accommodations could provide for at once), we had had the pleasure all day of being passed by equestrians and teams, and now as we mounted the slight hill on which the hotel tents were

The first hotel in Yellowstone National Park.
YELLOWSTONE HERITAGE AND RESEARCH CENTER.

placed we found ourselves the last of a numerous party and no welcome addition. The caravanserai at Norris consisted of half a dozen tents: one for the dining room, one for kitchen, and four for sleeping; and all told, drivers included, there were seventy of us there that night.

The accommodations were ludicrously insufficient and all who could provide for themselves at once withdrew. Among these were our two fellow passengers, a gentleman and his wife. Guided by Isaac they found a tolerable camping place, ate a hastily cooked supper, setup their three yards of canvas and crawled in. "Miss A." and myself, however, had no tent, and relied upon the overtasked resources of Norris. But where did all the seventy come from? There were many parties in the park and they all focused that night at Norris. It had been the plan of the park authorities that the best accommodations should be reserved for the Hatch party, but a high "military dignitary" had stolen a march upon them, gotten there first and had taken possession of at least one tent for the accommodation of his ladies. When therefore the Hatch party arrived great was their dissatisfaction to find even the poor accommodations that had been promised them not at their command.

"How and where shall I sleep?" became the important question. Miss A. and I at once resigned all hope of decent accommodation, thankful if only we were not left utterly shelterless. There fortune favored us and we found a most agreeable fellow sufferer in an English lady, a Miss Neave. She was one of those independent single women of wealth and position determined to see foreign countries, not after the goldfish fashion. With her own servants she had been camping in the park for a month. She had pitched her tents or "broken camp" as fancy dictated, staying till fully satisfied in favored spots. How we envied her! It is the only true way to see the park.

We three "lone women" made common cause, and the host of the "grand hotel," as soon as supper was cleared away, informed us that he would give us a corner of the dining tent, but he had no other accommodation to offer. In this same tent fifteen gentlemen were to sleep. They were busy arranging their blankets when we went in. Some had two, and indulged in the luxury of a blanket beneath as well as above them. Handbags in hand and each with her blanket, we marched to our appointed corner. The host (poor driven man) was graciousness itself. "Ladies if you have any pins I will put up a curtain for you." The pins were provided but the curtain, a dirty piece of burlap, was "as odd as Dick's hatband" (that went half-way round and tucked under). It left the broad side wholly exposed. "Here, ladies, is a pillow for you," and with these encouraging words he hauled out from beneath a crude bench (where it had been partly on the bare ground and partly on a quarter of beef) a very dirty burlap sack full, he said, of potatoes! After these princely acts of hospitality he left us to our slumbers.

August 24—Having got through the night the next thing was how to make a toilet. Alas! no conventionalities, no decencies for us that morning. I appealed to our English friend, Miss Neave. "Shake yourself like a donkey—that is all you can do," said she, and as an old campaigner I felt that she knew.

Seeing no possible chance of even a tin basin to myself (no not even a mug of water), I took a courage and cloth in hand and advanced to the wash bench. "Will you please sir pour a little water over this cloth for me?" The nearest gentleman obliged me, with my wet cloth I rubbed off my face and fingertips, and my toilet was made. My hair was not touched from my rising of one day at the Hot Springs till my going to bed of the next at the Upper Geyser Basin! After such a night stimulants were much in demand. Miss A. and I had a mere vial of brandy, but we were glad enough to have recourse to it and offered some to Miss Neave. She declined, brandy not being her "tipple," but went off into the kitchen where she got hot water and condensed milk and came back with a whiskey punch, which she kindly shared with us. There was no getting through such an experience without frequent "little goes" of strong waters. One English lady of the Hatch party came up to Miss Neave and seemed solicitous of a closer acquaintance with her. Miss N. was polite but cool and when said lady retired remarked to us, "That person is of what we call the tradesman class in England." Wasn't that English? But Miss Neave was right—the English of the Hatch Party were certainly not highbred.

The Norris Geyser Basin is on the headwaters of the Gibbon River, one of the branches of the Madison. From the road we survey it, a square mile or so of hot springs and geyser-like action. We look down upon a valley that seems all boiling water, mud puffs, embryo geysers, etc. just crusted over with a sheet of geyserite and looking exceedingly treacherous. They say explorers have ventured there, but I wouldn't for any money.

Our next stage was to Marshall's on the forks of the Firehole River. To reach this we went through Gibbon Canyon, the rocks often towering above us but neither so narrow nor so dark as to be very impressive. In some places the rocks encroach so that the road is in the river, but only for a short distance. Wherever one goes in the park boiling springs may be found. There is one close to the Gibbon River, so close that it is difficult to get by it. A team that we met there had come to grief—at least one of the horses certainly had. The poor creature had fallen not into the springs mud but into a quagmire that the escaping hot waters had made in the road. I hope it did not find its involuntary bath very hot. At any rate it was a warning to us. Passengers got out and picked our way across while Isaac managed the safe navigation of his team. Another team more luckless was almost wrecked and we had to help them right themselves. Often the road is so narrow that precautions have to be taken a mile ahead to prevent the meeting of teams where it would be impossible to pass.

We constantly met the most rustic of vehicles drawn by the roughest of farm animals and filled by the genuine sons and daughters of the soil. It was really strange to see how perfectly this class appreciates the wonders of the place and how glad they were to leave for a while their hard labor for the adventurous, the beautiful and the sublime.

So we went on a rather monotonous day's journey till the early afternoon brought us to the Forks of Firehole—Marshall's. This time we only stop to lunch and bait the horses. Marshall is a man who having no permit has chosen to assume that he could keep such a house of entertainment, that the Park Improvement Company would be glad to let him stay. When only rough teamsters and hunters visited the park I suppose he gave satisfaction. But now the crowds that throng there are of a more fastidious sort Marshall won't do. Marshall must go. The effective force here was only three—Marshall, his wife, and a Chinaman—and they are all overworked and all cross. Not being forethoughted or forehanded as to providing and not having very high standards I cannot praise their results.

A detachment of the Hatch Party had preceded us and eaten up everything clean, except some dry imported baker's bread and some poor cake. After a wearisome delay we managed to get some not very hot water with which we made some "Lieby's Extract" beef tea from our own stores. As we crumbled the baker's bread into this we were charged fifty cents apiece. We left as soon as possible.

The first thing that informed us that we were nearing our destination was a geyser in full blast. It was close to the river just where we had to cross it by a bridge (you may imagine boiling water is not good for horses' feet). It was the Riverside Geyser firing away across the river at an angle. If the wind sets directly towards the bridge there is no getting over till the performance is ended—10 to 13 minutes. It goes off three times a day.

After this every step revealed new wonders. The formations of world-renowned geysers—the Giant, the Castle, the Grotto, etc. were around us but I am sorry to say they were not in active operations, only spurting a little water in sprays, or throwing up an inconsiderable amount of steam. The sun was disappearing when we found ourselves before the semi-circle of tents—between twenty and thirty that formed the company's hotel. Back, hidden from ours by a tongue of pines, was the president's encampment.

The hotel manager came forward cordially and, after a few moments of puzzled thought, took us to a tent that was to be all our own. I could but exclaim (after our experience at Norris), "Palatial magnificence!" We were put in complete possession of a 13-by-16-foot tent with a roughhewn wooden door fastened by a button inside and with a string to wind round a nail outside, when ladies were "not at home." It had a bright-striped hemp carpet tacked all round to the lowest bar of its frame and a good mattress bed on the floor with a white honeycomb quilt. The washstand was a rough packing box, but it was furnished with a pitcher and basin, plenty of soft geyser water, soap and two towels.

We heard a "Swooop!" and "There he goes." It was dear Old Faithful—the never disappointing, the beautiful, the grand, the typical geyser. Mr. Hobart drew aside the tent curtain and there, not an eighth of a mile away, towered in the rosy evening light the clean shaft, the fearless column. For a while we could only look and exclaim; the display lasted some five or six minutes. There are others, geysers that rise higher, much, but for all practical purposes this is enough; and as you start back in dread and awe, the 130 or 140 feet is just as grand as if it were 200 or more. Then Faithful rises so straight and clean, uninterfered with by side spurts and splashings, that he is really the perfect geyser. Bless him! He is so entirely all that we had anticipated and was so reliable, playing for us every hour that we learned to love him.

In my guidebook I read that the little pools around Old Faithful have "pink and yellow margins and being constantly wet the colors are 'beautiful beyond description'." Then all I can say is that I must be colorblind. I could see a faint ashes of rose tint, a pearly gray, and the tawny yellow of iron rust, but "brilliant beyond description" makes one imagine vivid greens, intense yellows, clear blues, flaming scarlets, and flowing crimsons; and I saw none of these.

After Old Faithful the most satisfactory sight was the Sawmill Geyser. It erupted several times during the two hours, from twenty to thirty minutes at a time, with a regular kind of throb that at a little distance sounds like a sawmill. It kindly gave us one of its most beautiful exhibitions. It rises from a lovely blue pool. It throws up not a shaft but a full fountain not more than thirty feet. But the water is so beautifully broken into large drops that flash like diamonds in the sun that while the performance lasts it is impossible to turn away. Lingering about, in hopes of seeing the Grand, we saw the Sawmill twice.

Early in the afternoon we were obliged to leave and journey back to Marshall's. We had a tolerably good supper, which I enjoyed. Part of the reason was that our party got in early and the over-worked cook was not so rushed. We had fish nicely fried and quite tolerable coffee. I often found it difficult when things were at their worst to force down enough to sustain nature, such abominable messes were served up to us.

Above the square part of the building was a great loft, and this was elegantly subdivided into cells by burlap partitions reaching rather more than halfway up. Judging by their size there must have been more than a dozen of these little cubbyholes. Into these most of us were stowed.

Our room was in the southeast corner upstairs and had two beds in it, one at each end. Mrs. Gobeen was our roommate. It fell to my lot to sleep where the eaves came down over me like the crust over the blackbird in the pie. Mrs. Gobeen objected to having the window open. The bed was stuffed with sagebrush and had a horrid medicinal, quininey smell. And though the bedclothes may have been clean, I fancied that they had every teamster in the valley, besides being washed in that hot spring till the blankets were perfect felt. Moreover, with the sagacity usually exhibited by the lower classes in bed making, every double blanket had its fold up towards the head, so that if you were too warm you had to throw off both thicknesses or neither.

It was the morning of Monday August 27 that we were to leave Marshall's for the falls, striking off in a northeasterly direction from the north and south course. How long it seemed before we could get Isaac started! Our fresh team went off at a round pace, the little black mule doing particularly good service. Our serenity was restored and we gave ourselves up to such enjoyment as we could get out of our long hot dusty ride. What a view! Here and there, near and far, clouds of steam rising through the dark pines told of concealed wonders never to be enjoyed by us, while all around rose the mountains. It was at noon camp in Hayden Valley that we gathered fir cones and made fire to boil our coffee and cook our eggs. Strange, what a flavor there is to such simple experiences. I shall always love the spot even though I will never see it again.

Somewhere on this route Isaac pointed to the turning that led to Yellowstone Lake—only fourteen miles off and we could not go! It made us heartsick. We had neither the time nor the money it would have required, nor were there any public accommodations there.

Tuesday, August 28—The sun was not as high as it should have been to show the Lower Falls to the best advantage, but it was enough. It was all perfectly wild and untouched nature and grandeur unsurpassed.

Niagara is the standard by which all cataracts are judged. Well, this was not Niagara with its immensity of volume and power, but the general feeling was that in everything else the Lower Fall was greatly the superior. The setting was so superb—the dark green of the pines, the emerald green of the water, the white foam of the broken masses, and the wonderful, wonderful canyon. Then from the fall, the river dashed wildly away, like a hurt thing and down, down in the bottom of the canyon it looked so frenzied that it no longer seemed merely water. We looked at it from a height of 1,875 feet sheer depth! But the Falls and the Canyon! How could we turn away and leave them after such a mere glimpse? The sun every instant shone more directly into the canyon, fairly illuminating it. We all agreed that earth could not furnish another such beautiful sight. I shall never forget it. How thankful I am to Miss Abbott for getting me there! I think we stood on the very spot from which my very best stereographs were taken.

We had to go; for we had to reach Marshall's again that night. By eleven o'clock we had set out on our return journey. There were a few objects of interest that in our haste the evening before we had left unvisited. We stopped for a short time at Sulphur Mountain, apparently a mass of sulphur enclosed in a thin shell of geyserite.

Wednesday, August 29—We had no geyserial premonitions that night at Marshall's to disturb our slumbers and we were getting used to quininey mattresses and smelly felted blankets. We slept well, were very willing to see the last of that place.

Fifteen miles brought us to Norris where under the trees we took our last lunch. About one o'clock we resumed our journey. This last stage was tiresome in the extreme. It promised nothing to break the monotony.

We were within the last five miles of Mammoth when we entered upon the descent of Terrace Mountain. A cloud that had added to the beauties of sunset suddenly grew threatening. It rapidly spread over the sky and rain began to fall. It was now quite dark, and how cheery the bright lights of the hotel looked! Oh! At last! We were there! At the sound of our wheels, various officials rushed out with umbrellas to assist us to dismount and to help us up the rather ladder-like steps of the grand entrance, for all who have made the tour of the park are expected to return half dead, spent, and powerless.

Soaping Geysers to Make Them Play

Georgina M. Synge—1889

Georgina M. Synge was an English writer who published a small book about her trip to Yellowstone Park in 1892, but her trip was in 1889. She traveled to the park with her husband (she just called him "A.") by train to central Idaho and from there on horseback through the park's west entrance. Georgina could have gone to the park's northern entrance and taken a five-day hotel tour, but preferred camping out, traveling at her own pace, and breaking the rules now and then.

Her trip is a good example of the kind of Yellowstone Park tour by well-heeled tourists who could afford to buy camping equipment and horses and wagons as well as hire drivers, cooks, and guides. The trips were marked contrasts to those of "sagebrushers," who provided for all their own needs, or "Wylie Way" campers, who were driven in comfortable coaches by knowledgeable drivers and stayed in comfortable tents that were equipped with stoves and wooden floors.

Georgina was intrigued by the differences between England and America and wrote delightful descriptions of the colorful characters she met including trappers and prospectors. She relished the excellent fishing, described the bears and other animals she saw and sneaked out one night to drop soap down Beehive Geyser to force it to play (a strategy that doesn't work). She provides marvelous descriptions of the sights she saw, and the adventures she had.

Here a condensed version of Georgina's book, A Ride Through Wonderland, *Sampson Low, Makstone & Company, London, 1892.*

* * * *

We made sundry inquiries before we set out on our tour as to the best end by which to reach the park. Nearly everyone advised us to take the Mammoth Springs entrance, as the Northern Pacific Railway runs a branch line to Cinnabar, only six miles distant.[1] As, however, we intended coming up from Salt Lake by the Utah Northern, we decided to enter the other end from Beaver Canyon, which, although 115 miles from the park, is the nearest point the railway touches. This route leads through a delightfully wild and unfrequented country, abounding most of the way with game, and for those who can spare the time it is well worth the extra journey.

We procured the greater part of our stores at Salt Lake, laying in enough to last ourselves and two men for about a fortnight. We made our purchases at the Mormon Co-operative Stores, and found all our "saintly" food most satisfactory. We were served by a modest young Mormon, who told us he had been employed in the Army and Navy Stores in London before he became a saint, but found the Mormon hours, and holidays, and pay, more satisfactory; also doubtless the choice of wives, though he did not mention this.

Beaver Canyon is the funniest little place. As we had to wait there three days to collect our outfit (and scour the country for a sidesaddle, an article which we had foolishly omitted to bring), we had plenty of time for observation. It stands between two low ridges of hills which form the entrance to the Canyon, and consists of several rows of little wooden houses and a few rather larger ones "dumped" here and there on its brown treeless level. Enormous signboards announced that a large percentage of these mansions were "restaurants" and "beer saloons." The hotel is decidedly primitive, and as the air does not seem to suit either cows or hens, the luxuries produced by these useful species come from a distance, and are rather scarce. The railway runs through the middle of the town, and, as there is no road (and only one or two trains in the day), forms the fashionable resort of the inhabitants on Sundays and fine evenings. One great drawback to enjoying this, however, is that one's eyes have to be more or less glued to one's footsteps, as the sleepers are raised rather high above the ground, and a glance upwards may land one upon one's nose.

The day before we started, our horses were brought round for us to try. As my sidesaddle had not arrived, and having terrible stories of bucking "cayuses" in my mind, I must confess I felt some trepidation on mounting my wiry-looking little beast, and having to sit helplessly sideways on the big

---

1 The Northern Pacific promoted the northern entrance to the park as the best way to see the park, claiming it gave visitors a sequence of sights of increasing spectacle culminating with the canyon and falls of the Yellowstone River.

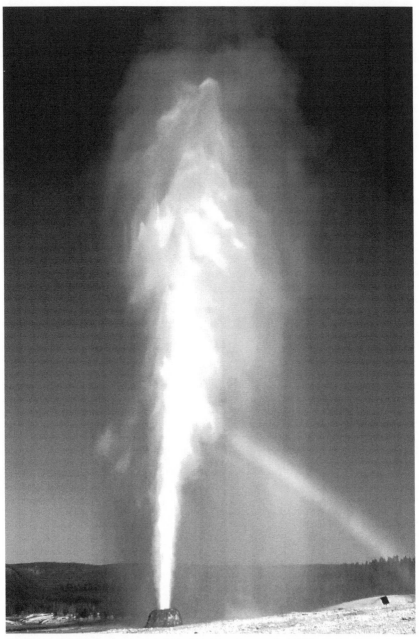

Georgina Synge dropped soap into Beehive Geyser in 1892 under the now debunked theory that it would force it to play.
NATIONAL PARK SERVICE.

Mexican saddle. However, "Bolly" turned out of most lamb-like demeanor, and I "loped" him up and down under the critical eyes of a group of cowboys who were sitting on some wooden doorsteps, chewing straws, and surveying us with rather disdainful glances.

A's horse, "Snip," was more of an Eastern build than the others, which were cayuses. He was rounder in the barrel, and much less weedy-looking, and though not quite so sure -footed, was a very good goer. The guide rode a big raw-boned beast of wonderful enduring powers, but which bucked steadily for five minutes each time he was mounted, a considerable drawback in our unaccustomed eyes. Then there were two stout animals, a roan and a grey, to draw the wagon, a vehicle on half springs covered with canvas, something like a grocer's cart.

We got all our outfit together at last, Messrs. Bassett Bros., who run the stages through the park reservation, supplying us at about seventeen dollars per day. This included the hire and forage of the horses, a guide, a lad to drive the wagon, a tent, and cooking utensils, etc.

A. was for taking no mattress—"roll yourself up in a rug, and there you are," was his idea. But as I ventured to differ as to the delights of this method, we ended by procuring huge bags filled with fresh hay, which were most comfortable. We also took about eight blankets and a mackintosh cover. A small leather portmanteau contained our changes of raiment and toilet necessaries, also such useful things as tools, fishing gear, and a few simple ointments and medicines. My costume was peculiar, as it had to be adapted to walking and climbing as well as horseback. It consisted of riding trousers and high leather leggings, a very short tweed skirt, a crimson flannel blouse, and a cowboy's felt hat to keep off the sun. We each wore a leather belt with pockets, containing collapsible drinking cups, compasses, knives and string, etc., which we found a great comfort.

As for our food, we took a good load of tinned beef and tongue, sardines, flour, biscuits, bacon, coffee, cracked wheat, tinned milk and fruit, and a bottle of Worcester sauce (without which no American table is complete); also two bottles of whiskey and a box of Mormon beer, "in case," as A. remarked, "the water might be injurious."

We started on the first of September—a glorious day. A brilliant sun and crisp fresh air, every breath of which felt like a tonic. We set forth early in the morning, as we had about thirty miles to ride before reaching a good camping ground. This first thirty miles is the least interesting part of the way, though its wide undulating sweeps covered thickly with sagebrush, with here and there a solitary group of pine or aspen standing bleak against the sky, have a fascination of their own, and seemed to us a fitting entrance to the weird and wonderful land beyond.

All among this sagebrush on each side of us were innumerable badger holes, terrible to behold; and though A. and Snip made frequent short cuts, I, having a distinct aversion to breaking my neck needlessly, kept steadily to the trail. It is wonderful, though, how knowing the Western horses are in avoiding these dangerous pitfalls. Bolly always seemed to keep a sharp look out, and would give an indignant little snuff of disapprobation on passing near one; and as he never by any chance put his foot into them, I grew quite resigned to even "loping" over them at last.

Beesley, the guide, was inclined to be rather morose and taciturn, but Jim, the lad who drove the wagon, was quite the reverse, and told us all his family history as he cooked our lunch. He informed us he always liked "doin' the thing" with English folk; they weren't mean like the Yanks, who grudged you every bite you took. After this pleasing eulogy, of course, I hadn't a word to say on discovering that a little basket of pears, brought for my special refection, and placed in a corner of the wagon, was nearly empty!

How delicious that first meal was, free from all the humdrum conventionalities of life, surrounded by wild stretches of country, with not a human habitation or sign of human life visible.

Our bread was baked in a small cast iron Dutch-oven, something like a gipsy's kettle, the edges of the cover being turned up to hold the hot embers; I never tasted bread more excellent. In this oven, too, we could cook our meat or fish. The men always ate with us, quite at home and at their ease, as we sat together on the wagon seats round our little camp table. For when you come Far West every man is as good as another, and everybody you meet is a "gentleman," whether it is the boy who blacks your boots or the rich man who owns his millions. I must say we found them most well mannered and agreeable (with the exception of Beesley, whom we afterwards changed), and most eager that we should see everything we could.

My horse seemed to me very rough at first, and the saddle not all that might be desired, with its sharp little pummels and generally antiquated structure; but I soon became accustomed to both, and Bolly's steady "lope," kept up mile after mile as if he were propelled by clockwork, was really much less fatiguing for long distances than the uncertain paces of an Eastern horse. In these regions, too, horses are all bitted with a single rein on a very sharp curb, so that the merest touch is sufficient to control them. Indeed, the reins seem very little used, and are often left hanging quite loose, all the guiding being done by knee pressure.

We reached our first camping ground, in the Camas Meadows—brown grass-covered levels surrounded by mountains—by about five o'clock in the afternoon. We chose a snug spot on the lee of a small hill covered with clumps of fir and close to a dear little icy-cold spring, which bubbled out of the earth, edged with a winding green fringe of grass to mark its course along the burnt-up ground.

What fun it was pitching our tent for the first time, and gathering wood for a huge camp fire, and picketing the horses, and exploring our surroundings, and discovering a little forsaken "dug-out" on the hill-side, a sort of hole scooped in the earth, and roofed with branches, the temporary home of some prospector or pioneer.

We slept like tops, nor did we feel the least cold, though our sponges were frozen hard the next morning. We were awakened by a little chipmunk, a sort of tiny squirrel (not much larger than a mouse), that jumped about on the top of our tent uttering shrill little cries. Nearly everywhere we stopped we had these curious little creatures peeping in and out amongst our things, moved evidently with a violent curiosity, and quite untroubled by fears. They would come close up to us and would eat crumbs almost out of our hands, and they always were to be seen scampering about the horses' feet when they were having their corn, and would sit up so prettily, with their furry tails over their backs, and munch the scattered grains.

We started soon after breakfast on the second day, leaving the men to pack up and follow with the wagon. Gradually our surroundings were becoming more broken and hilly. Fresh ranges of mountains began to loom up on all sides, sometimes so clearly defined, their lights and shadows so distinct, that they appeared but a few miles off.

It was late in the evening when we caught a glimpse of the Snake River itself, silently hurrying, white and gleaming, through dark forest-covered banks to its awful distant leap. We splashed through its shallow bed, which here is easily forded, and drew up on the other side, near some log cabins built for the accommodation of passing travelers. Here the horses were indulged in the luxury of stables, and Jim, after some foraging, returned triumphantly with a pumpkin pie for our supper. We chose a charming spot amongst the trees for pitching our tent, close to the water and far enough away from the civilized settlement.

Having only ridden about sixteen miles that day we felt quite fresh, and so putting on wading boots, and getting out fishing rods and tackle, we sallied forth in quest of the wily trout. It was very lovely. We waded downstream about a mile, and had a delightful swim in the swift, cold waters, while the sun began to set behind the great black pine stems and bathed us in streaks of golden glory. But not a fish did we even see.

That night we made a grand bonfire, and as we were toasting ourselves over it (and listening to the howls of the coyotes), two guides from a passing stage, and a hunter, came up and began to chat with us. They seemed greatly interested in our movements, and gave us any amount of information about our route and what we ought to see. One of them was the best hunter in the place, and had just arrived with several elk and the skin of a fine cinnamon bear. He had been out with two gentlemen and a lady from California, and seemed to consider the lady the best shot of the party; at any rate two big elk had fallen to her share. The hunter with whom we had talked the evening before presented us with a huge elk steak as we took our departure that afternoon.

We only made about eight miles this time, the road winding for the first half of the way through thick woods. These, however, diminished gradually into clumps of trees dotted about over grassy slopes, and soon found ourselves again on the banks of the Snake. Here we camped and enjoyed a quiet evening, mending our already torn clothes, and attending to various details of our domestic economy.

Well, we had very fine sport the next day, the trout rising freely to a "yellow coachman," which seems a quite irresistible fly in these parts. Our old man made us promise to keep his happy hunting-ground a secret, though, while in those regions, as he complained very much of the way people ruthlessly destroyed the fish in other more frequented rivers, by dynamite and other foul means. "And they would soon empty our Snake if they could," he added, resentfully.

With two large bags of this excellent fish tied to our saddles we started on our way, the men having had orders to go some ten miles on and pitch our tent a little beyond the Lower Snake crossing. Unfortunately, we were obliged to wade the horses the whole way back to our late camping ground, owing to a tiresome deep hole in the bed of the Snake, which they absolutely refused to cross. This "doubling on our tracks" delayed us very much, and the sun had set as we turned at last into our proper course.

The whole of the next morning we were delayed by the horses, which, in spite of their hobbles, had managed to make off and could not be found. So, having enjoyed an excellent trout breakfast, we lay serenely on our backs in the shade, while the men scoured the country for the missing steeds. At last, after about five hours' search, the truants were discovered, and driven home.

We soon saddled up, and started on our way, having about seventeen miles to make to our next camping ground. The forest stretched in front of us for the first hour or so, but it soon became thinner and the view more open beyond, till suddenly, turning sharply round the bend of a hill, we saw before us a great open valley, level and grassy, and completely walled in on three sides by ranges of mountains. To the east, however, it extended as far as the eye could reach on to a limitless prairie, out of which the white round peaks of the Three Tetons towered majestically all by themselves some seventy miles away. Through this valley, some ten miles long, lay our road, at the upper extremity of which we could see a glittering speck, Henry's Lake, a favorite resort of the hunter and angler. Flocks of wild geese and countless heron were basking in this sunny valley, and a "bunch" of horses were browsing on the slopes beyond.

As we ascended the steep slopes of Targhee Pass, we kept turning back to admire the blue water of Henry's Lake, the abruptly rising banks of the Pass, covered with fir and maple, making an effective setting to the lovely, dreamy valley below; a contrast all the more striking as dark clouds were rapidly gathering in front of us and the wind was coming in fitful gusts down the Pass. It was extraordinary how quickly the storm gathered and how cold it became. As it was getting very dark we settled to camp at once, and chose the most sheltered spot we could find on the lee of a small hill. But we had to content ourselves with a very cold and fragmentary supper that evening, as our fire was soon blown out and our food blown away! The tent was by no means fitted to withstand a gale, and though we pegged it down as best we could, the wind puffed it in upon us like a balloon, and we had to put logs of wood on our blankets to keep them down. Every minute the storm increased, till, as we watched by the dim light of our lamp, it seemed to shake our canvas walls as if in the hands of a fury, and the pole swayed to and fro as if it was drunk.

"It's going," I shouted, after a fearful gust, but A., who has a wonderful faculty for taking a nap under trying circumstances, did not reply. Just for a moment there was a lull, but only for a moment; then there came a great roar, and in a twinkling the tent was torn from the ground and hurled into the air, our blankets and various belongings whirling after it. Luckily, however, we had not undressed, so we were not in so bad a plight as we might have been. The men had taken refuge in the wagon (they generally slept rolled in rugs under a tree); but on hearing what had happened, they turned out and we took their places, having first secured a few of our wraps and our hay bags from the boisterous elements. Luckily, the canvas cover to the wagon buttoned well round, and protected us from the rain and hail, which presently beat down upon us like an avalanche. We managed to keep pretty warm and comfortable, as we were wedged in between a sack of flour and the tinned meats. The men, quite undisturbed by such a small catastrophe, crept under the fallen tent, which they had recovered, and seemed to enjoy excellent repose, though, when we peeped out at about five a.m., nothing could be seen of them but a little white mound, as the whole ground was covered with snow. Anything more wintry, one could hardly imagine. White peaks enclosing us on every side, trees bowed down with snowy wreaths, and a dark leaden sky overhead. No wonder we had begun to feel rather chilly, in spite of having pulled over ourselves a saddle and some provisions! We could not help laughing, however, at the injured and pitiable group of horses we beheld standing: tails to storm, heads bowed down. Everything was soaking wet; the fire took a long time to light; and all our things had got more or less mixed up or blown away in the night. However, we maintained a cheerful equanimity, and before long were rewarded by seeing faint streaks of sunlight trying to pierce their way through the clouds; and by the time we were ready to start it was beaming forth gloriously, rapidly melting the snow and warming the chilly air.

We passed through several miles more forest that day—forests of black fir and spruce and of the tall white pine. On leaving them behind we entered upon vast grassy areas, from where could be seen far ahead the darkly timbered mountains which flank the Madison Valley to the east.

The Madison is one of the chief tributaries of the Missouri, and has its source in the Yellowstone Park, where it is called the Firehole River, rather appropriately, as it rises in the midst of geyser coves and boiling streams and springs.

We crossed the Madison and were once more among the forests; forests of the dead more than of the living. Long intervals were sometimes completely covered with fallen and decaying timber: a strange and melancholy sight. All the pines die on reaching a certain height, and drop or are blown down, sometimes one by one, sometimes in whole tracts at a time. There they lie, piled up upon each other in various stages of decay; some with long lines of dust only, to mark out their forms, while pushing young sproutlings are filling up their places and flaunting green shoots over the poor moldering remains.

Bolly, who would stand unmoved by the side of a geyser, thundering forth its two hundred feet of seething waters, had a distinct aversion to dead trees, and would shy most unexpectedly at some poor harmless looking fallen veteran, or gnarled old trunk that we passed.

Some halfway across the valley we came to the military camp, which is established at the western entrance to the park.[2] Here we were accosted by two soldiers in uniform, who asked us if we had any guns to declare, as, if we had, they must be sealed up, to prevent our using them while passing through. For one of the most stringent park laws is against molesting the game, or any animal within its limits; and though people are allowed to fish, they are supposed not to take more than is required for their party. If they are caught trespassing, they are promptly walked out from the nearest entrance, accompanied by a military escort, nor, under any pretext, will they be allowed to enter again. A very excellent law, and owing to its strict observance, the Yellowstone Park may be considered the animals' paradise. For here the almost exterminated buffalo can find a haven of safety, and the antelope and the elk, the big horned sheep and the mountain goat, can roam unmolested by bloodthirsty man. Even the bear too is not to be trifled with, and it seems quite a

---

2 The army took over administration of the park in 1886.

moot point if one is allowed to defend oneself from his embraces. We heard of a man who was caught in the act of shooting a grizzly within the limits, and who pleaded in defense that the grizzly had been stalking him, not he the grizzly, and as it had broken the rules by so doing, he was obliged to shoot it, as he could not walk it out of the park in any other way.

As a rule, however, the bear does not seem to hanker after human flesh, and, unless attacked, when it defends itself with unequalled ferocity and courage, appears to lead a very harmless life, feeding on wild fruits in the summer, and on game and any carrion it can find in the winter.

We were close now upon the great Divide, as this Rocky Mountain barrier is called, up which the road ascends in steep zigzags.

We had a grand panorama from the top. The Madison winding through the valley like a thin silver line. Vast forests, some dark masses of green; others, charred black wastes, or peeled and white like armies of ghosts. Broad flat levels, misty distant valleys, range behind range of blue and violet hills; and not a sign, not a vestige of human life visible.

As we descended the other side, the forest received us again and closed in upon us; a forest so dark and impenetrable, few rays of sunlight could ever find their way within. We were about four hours riding through this, and it was evening when we at last emerged upon the Fire Hole Basin. Here stands quite a little settlement, consisting of the "Hotel," the stage agent's house, and a few primitive abodes belonging to men employed there during the summer months.

We were too tired to do anything but eat a hearty supper, though the peculiar sulfurous smell in the air, showing how near we were to "Wonderland" at last, made us long for morning to come.

We started forth, full of anticipation, to explore early next day. The Lower Geyser Basin, as it is called, is covered with coarse grass, and is almost destitute of trees, although surrounded by them on every side. The geysers lie scattered about in groups, their presence plainly discernible by the cloudy wreaths of vapor which show up against the dark hills behind.

As we approached the geyser cones, the ground became quite bare and was covered with innumerable cracks and crevices, while the cones themselves and a few yards around them, appeared to be composed of pure white lime.

The first geyser we saw was the "Fountain," and though it only goes up about fifty feet—quite insignificant, compared with those in the Upper Basin—yet, it was our first, and thrilled us accordingly.

We tethered the horses to some stunted shrubs growing near, and stood eagerly watching while the "Fountain" began to boil up in preparation for action. The opening is in the center of a pool about fifty feet in diameter, and projects from a sort of mound of rounded cushion-like formation, in which is the great orifice.

An angry spirit seemed at work, the water was dashing violently upwards, and the whole pool covered with foam. Then suddenly it would cease, then would begin again more furiously than ever. At last it became quite full of madly tossing waters, and then finally with a great roar up they shot in a beautiful column of some forty or fifty feet.

It played for several minutes, then lowered its crest and faltered, then shot up again, and so on for about half an hour. At length it stopped; with plaintive groans and gurgles the water sank out of sight, and the basin was left quite empty, so that we could distinctly see the curious white sponge-like formation with which it was lined. Not far from the "Fountain" are some springs, the ground about which is of a blood-red color, caused by some low form of vegetable growth.

In the afternoon we went to see the "Queen's Laundry," another pool of boiling water, which overflows into a series of smaller basins, divided from each other by lovely coral-like ridges of white formation. The water is very soft, and gradually cools as it flows from one pool to another, so that one can take a bath, or wash anything if so disposed. We had brought one of A.'s flannel coats, which had acquired a good deal of grime by the way, and this we washed very successfully by dabbling it about in pools of various temperatures. A. was induced, under great pressure, to put it on and sit in the sun to dry when we got home, and this excellent method quite prevented it shrinking.

Alas, that evening on saddling up we found Bolly's back was wrung; we had feared this would be the case, as the saddle did not fit him, though we had been very careful to pad it with horse-cloths underneath. For long rides like this, unless one can be sure of one's saddle, it is better to ride astride. Only it is well to secure a small, light saddle, as the big Mexican ones are too wide for a woman. It is not unusual out West for women to ride this way, and it certainly makes it far easier for the horse. I tried it towards the end of our journey, thinking the change would be beneficial to my steed's back. As the good little beast "loped" pleasantly along most of the way, I found it very comfortable; but I cannot answer for what would have happened if he had bucked or shied.

Beesley shuffled up to our campfire that evening, and after a long silence and much spitting into the glowing embers, said he guessed he wasn't much good at bossing the park, and he wasn't going to do that anymore. This we felt was meant as an apology, so we wished him good luck, and parted quite amicably.

I was very sorry to change poor Bolly, but he certainly could not go any further, so the stage agent, with some difficulty, found another animal for us, a rather rough-looking beast, called Blaine, after the Minister of the Interior. This A. rode, I taking Snip, as he was the lighter of the two. We also made a change in guides, and were provided with an excellent pioneer, named Smithson, and his son Elijah, a lad of eighteen, to cook and drive the wagon.

There was a sharp frost that night, and the ice was quite thick in our pails, but as we were over 7,000 feet above the sea this was not surprising, and we were quite snug and warm in our tent, which we had had mended and patched up since the calamity of the night before.

We took an early swim in the Fire Hole River next morning; rather a curious experience, as it was quite warm, and very sulfurous. We were surveyed in speechless horror by some of the natives, who evidently considered us quite demented; and, indeed, Smithson afterwards affirmed he would rather face a grizzly than take a bath—at least a bath of that description. I do not think either he or Elijah ever took off their clothes the whole time they were with us. Certainly their toilet necessaries were extremely limited, and consisted of a mattress, two rugs, and half a comb, the latter kept jealously in Elijah's pocket, and lent to his father as occasion might require. Smithson, indeed, was much struck by all our luxuries. He did not at all approve of my sponge, saying it was a "ter'ble" thing to wash one's face in the park. However, I did not find my complexion any the worse; though, of course, one has to be careful and use plenty of Vaseline or cold cream, as the chemical ingredients in the water, and the alkali dust combined, are apt to cause irritation to the skin.

We started for the Great Geyser Basin about ten o'clock, forded the river, and following the road which led through the Fire Hole Valley, for about five miles, came to the Egeria Spring, better known, however, as "Hell's Half Acre." For here lies "Excelsior," the largest and most powerful geyser in the world, the thunder of whose eruptions can be heard for miles around; which sends up its boiling contents to a height of 300 feet, hurling huge rocks to all sides, as if they were pebbles, and flooding the river with such volumes of water that the bridges are sometimes swept away.

But alas, "Excelsior" did not play for us. This monster geyser seems to take long intervals of repose, sometimes not erupting for several years. It had been very active the summer before (1888), and so was now resting from its labors. Smithson remarked to us for consolation, that it was such a "ter'ble" thing when that did "guise" we should all "wish we was in kingdom come."

We tied our horses to some trees, and crossed the white chalky formation to where "Excelsior" lies, some 200 yards from the trail. Even in repose the giant geyser looked very awe-inspiring. It was belching forth volumes of steam, and as the wind wafted this to one side, we could look down into its great open mouth, some 250 feet in diameter, and about 30 feet deep. The water at the bottom was furiously boiling, and the edges of the huge caldron were jagged, and in many places undermined. Large masses keep continually falling in, and each year it gets larger and larger. Towards the river end the sides slope downwards, taking the shape of the hill over which the waters, streaming, and spreading, form terraces of a lovely rose and orange tint.

But if "Excelsior" is somewhat horrible, a few yards off lies a sight so entrancingly beautiful one feels that Hell's Half Acre contains an element of Heaven. This is a large pool called the Grand Prismatic Spring. Its surface is quite calm and unruffled, and its colors are indescribably lovely.

In the center it is a wonderful dark deep blue, changing nearer the edge to a vivid green. Around the rim it fades into yellow—into orange—a ring of red—then purplish grey, the colors being intensified by the white coral-like deposit with which the pool is lined. One's eyes revel in these glorious hues, as they melt one into another, the whole glistening in its pure white setting like a liquid jewel.

But even lovelier was the Turquoise Pool, which lies close beside its Prismatic sister. It is about 100 feet square, and is of a blue so exquisite, so deep, so pure, the very sky—brilliant and unclouded, and thought so blue before—looked dark and colorless now. We stood fascinated. In its limpid transparency we could see every detail of the pearly shell-like formation beneath.

No alabaster could be whiter, no sculpture more delicate than the curious wreathing devices, and foliations, which clustered round the rim. The overflow had worn a little channel, as it trickled down the slope, and enameled it with pink, and orange, and yellow. It was fairy-like and it was weird. For a background were forests looking dark and cold against the white chalky plateau on which we were standing; while here and there around us stood poor white ghosts of dead pine, stretching out bare despairing arms,—punished for their temerity in daring to take root near the great Excelsior.

We had only about six miles to ride before reaching the Upper Geyser Basin, and the road wound pleasantly over wooded knolls, and pretty sweeps of valley, misty columns of vapor rising up, like water wraiths from various boiling pools and baby geysers on every side. At last we emerged upon this Great Geyser Basin.

The Grotto was "guising"—the popular mode of expressing an eruption—as we entered the valley, and we hurried up to get a good view. The water was shooting upwards in two jets, from its grotto-like cone which stands about eight feet high, with a curious pillar on one side; and two little infant geysers were vigorously spurting away a few feet from it. The ground all around is covered with beaded silica which breaks up in slabs if disturbed. We looked down into the Grotto's curious arched cavities after it had ceased playing, lined with a smooth pearly formation, and into the black depths of its great funnel-shaped orifices, and wondered as to the extent of the terrible power beneath, to which it acts as a safety valve.

At the upper end of the geyser basin stands a most civilized-looking hotel in Queen Anne style, and quite a sprinkling of people rather elaborately attired for such a remote portion of the globe; one of them, clad in an elegant velvet dolman, high-heeled shoes and much curled fringe, regarded my buckskin leggings through her pince-nez with cold and withering glances. Indeed, my appearance I found quite attracted people's attention from the geysers. I suppose if I had worm a blue plush habit with a locket and ribbon bow—as I saw a western damsel disporting herself in one day—I should have attracted no notice at all.

That afternoon I unwittingly came within the iron grasp of the law. We had sallied forth after lunch for a geyser exploration, and I was looking into the pretty little cone of one of the "Cubs" which stand on each side of their big parent, the "Lioness" (so named because of the growling noise they make). This dear little "Cub" was boiling away at a great pace inside its pretty raised marble rim, and having heard what capita] wash-tubs geysers made, I dropped in my handkerchief, and was quite absorbed in watching it being sucked down and then thrown up again, then sucked town to reappear once more. Suddenly a hand was laid on my shoulder, and a stern voice remarked, "Do you know you are breaking the rules?" A., who had been quite lost in contemplating the "Lioness," now hurried up, and we both explained we had no idea washing handkerchiefs was included in the rules, and we repented deeply and would never offend again, etc. The man was evidently mollified and assured us that he was only doing his duty, and that that very morning a party had been marched out for throwing some eggs into "Old Faithful" to be boiled. However, he consented not to report us, and even condescended to try and rescue the erring handkerchief with my stick, which the "Cub," in a fright no doubt, had swallowed down and refused to eject. We poked about for some while and at last had to relinquish it, time being precious. We had not gone very far, however, when we heard someone running after us, and lo and behold! there was our good "Jonathan" quite out of breath, and holding up the handkerchief—washed snowy white—which he said the "Cub" had just disgorged.

We heard rather an amusing story of an Englishman (it would have been an American in England, I suppose) new to geyserland, who had had rather an unpleasant experience of one of the "Cubs." He had sat down upon the cone of one of them to wait for the "Lioness" to play, and as she did not seem inclined to hurry, he took a nap. Suddenly the "Cub" went off, after a few premonitory growlings, which he did not hear, and sent him flying from his seat, very much scalded and nearly frightened out of his wits.

We feasted on geysers all that afternoon. The "Castle," a pile of about twenty feet, looking something like a ruined fortress, which stands on a mound of grey and white deposit, went off splendidly. This is supposed once to have been the most powerful geyser in the Upper Basin, but though it sends up a vast mass of water and clouds of steam, it does not go higher than about fifty feet.

A little beyond the "Castle" is the "Morning Glory," a pool of a lovely pale blue, quite round and deepening in the center, and with lovely white petal-like edges. Then there was the "Oblong' that threw itself up in a great splashing mass every four or five hours from with beautiful deep green pool.

And the "Sawmill," which sent up a pretty little jet every few minutes with a noise like a sawmill working in a desperate hurry. The "Fan," too, is very pretty during eruption, spreading out in graceful fan-shaped fountains, and the sun shining through the falling spray gives an effect of showers of pearls.

Though we waited and longed, neither the "Splendid" nor the "Grand," which go up over two hundred feet, would perform for us. The "Giantess," which sends up the largest mass of water after "Excelsior," plays very seldom now. It is said to double the quantity of water in the river with its overflow, and goes up two hundred and fifty feet in one terrific ebullition.

But the geyser we set our hearts on seeing was the "Beehive," just opposite our camp, the other side of the basin. The cone, which really has all the appearance of a beehive in the distance, is about three feet in height and is beautifully coated with beaded silica. Its action is different to any other geyser, as the water is projected with such force from its comparatively small vent-hole, that it goes up in one perfectly straight pillar to over two hundred feet; and, instead of falling in floods on each side like the others, seems to evaporate into wreaths of steam and vapor.

Now there is a sure and almost certain method for inducing a geyser to play out of its accustomed hours, and this is done by what is called "soaping" them! It may sound incredible, but it is a well-known fact (which we attested on several occasions) that a bar or two of common yellow soap, cut up into pieces and slipped into a geyser cone, will have the desired effect in a very short interval. This is supposed to be partly caused by the soap creating a film on the water, which prevents the steam escaping. Smithson was as keen as we were that the "Beehive" should play. He assured us he had seen it soaped over and over again, with the most brilliant results.

So that night we sallied forth after all the world had gone to bed, armed with two large bars of Brown Windsor tied up in a pocket-handkerchief. The moon was shining fitfully behind the clouds, and now and then gleamed forth upon us, as, having crossed the river, we climbed up the white sloping sides of the "Beehive."

It was not due to play for several days, and as we peered down its dark funnel like orifice, we could hear a soft peaceful gurgling, but nothing more; and even this quite ceased after we had slipped in the soap. We sat down then and watched. Presently it began to boil up—little by little—with a buzzing sort of noise as if it were hard at work. Every now and then it threw up a few squirts of water, and Smithson, who was getting very excited, laid his "bottom dollar" it was going to play. But, alas, though it seemed to be trying with all its might, yet it never quite got off, and having watched for nearly an hour, we decided to send Smithson back to camp for some more soap. Perhaps we had not put in enough, we thought, though Smithson assured us two bars was all it had ever wanted before. Well, in went the second lot, but with just the same result. It showed all the premonitory symptoms, boiled over, made a few gasps, and sent up a few small jets, and then gave it up. We got quite desperate at last. It was nearly twelve o'clock, and very cold, as a sharp frost had set in. We thought, however, we would have one more try. We hurried back to camp. There we found Elijah, stretched fast asleep before the smoldering embers of the fire. We cruelly awoke him, and made him produce the last piece of yellow bar, which we had hitherto thought necessary to leave for washing purposes. And to augment this, A. insisted on my bringing forth our few and treasured cakes of Pears. But no, even this last sacrifice was of no avail—that "Beehive" would not play! Smithson was furious, the first time it had ever refused for him; someone must have soaped it the day before, and if only we would wait it was sure to begin soon. But we decided we could not freeze there all night, even to see the "Beehive" display; and so dejectedly we made our way once more back to camp. Just as we were going off to sleep we heard a roar—something was "guising" at last, but we were too tired to stir even if it had been "Excelsior." The next morning, however, just as we were dressed, we heard the roar again, like the sound of a sudden hurricane or of numberless distant guns. "She's off—the 'Beehive's guisin'," shouted Smithson, and off we dashed, helter-skelter, arriving breathless, but in capital time to see a grand eruption.

It was terrific. It seemed as if the whole hillside must be blown out by the tremendous force with which it burst forth. Higher and higher it soared, in one great round perpendicular column of over two hundred feet, clouding the whole sky with masses of spray and steam. Presently a gust of wind blew up and carried the topmost wreaths in feathery masses over the valley, and we were able to stand quite close to lee of it without getting a drop upon us. It played for about twenty minutes, then wavered, trembled, and finally subsided with sundry gurgles and groans. As we came away, several people who had hurried out from their beds to see the sight began making remarks on the curious fact of the "Beehive" playing before its proper time. "That's been soaped," said a man who belonged to the place, looking suspiciously round, at which we appeared innocently surprised.

We had to retrace our steps to the Fire Hole Basin to regain the trail or Yellowstone Lake, therefore we decided to camp at the former place that night, as our next resting place was to be on the banks of the Yellowstone River, nearly thirty miles distant. There were several lovely spots we should have liked to visit; Kepler's Cascades, about two miles east of the Upper Basin, where the water dashes through a deep, rugged, and very narrow canyon; and Shoshone Lake, lying in a hollow between heavily timbered hills; but we had to limit ourselves somewhere.

We made an early start next day, and had a good bit of hard climbing, as we had to cross the high "Divide" or range of hills, through which, further on, the Yellowstone Canyon is cut. On each side of us lay dead and prostrate pine, crammed in masses among the living, forming a very labyrinth of desolation. Through a gap amongst them, now and then, we caught a glimpse of the lovely bluish-purple Rockies, the higher peaks white with snow. Near the summit we passed a dear little lonely piece of water, called Mary's Lake, its edges strewed with fallen pine. We also passed Sulphur Lake, from which a very nasty odor arose, and further on Alum Creek, which our horses, though very thirsty, sniffed disdainfully and would not taste.

The other side of the Divide was undulating table-land, and here again were those curious park-like effects, and for miles we passed in and out of grassy slopes, surrounded by impenetrable woods, not once seeing a living creature larger than a chipmunk, though Smithson said the place was full of bear, and we came across buffalo and elk trails continually.

We were very anxious to see some big game, "roaming in their native forests free," and so Smithson proposed we should make a detour some miles off the trail, as we should then be more likely to see some. But not for all the "big game" in the world would I go that detour again.

First of all we stuck in a swamp, A.'s horse going in up to his girths, and Smithson's roan pitching him head over heels in its struggles into the black mud and rank grass which surrounded us. As for me, seeing their fate, I slid off Snip just in time as his forelegs sunk suddenly, up to his nose, in the treacherous ground. We floundered about for some minutes, and at last succeeded in dragging the frightened beasts on to terra firma; and the next mile or two, by skirting close to the trees, we managed to keep clear of pitfalls.

But swamps were mild compared to the terrors of the tracts of white chalky formation we had to cross. Boiling pools of sulphur all around us, steam belching up from the hoof-marks of our horses, as each step broke through the thin crust, while horrible groans and rumblings filled the air. It was all very well in the geyser basins, where the ground was hard and well tried by other feet. But here it was more than probable no human being had ever penetrated, or at any rate very few. Snip did not like it at all, and trembled with fright, as every step nearly sunk him over the fetlocks in the hot mud. I gathered a little comfort from the fact that A., who turns the scales at nearly twice my weight, was on in front, and, therefore, what bore him might be supposed to bear me. But all I know is that it did not, and that Snip and I had a horrid flounder in the steaming mud, near a wicked-looking gurgling hole, which the others passed quite safely. After that, being hot and thirsty we (Snip and I) nearly killed ourselves by drinking out of a lovely little purling stream, only Smithson rushed up just in time and said it was full of arsenic.

We were rather disreputable-looking objects, when we emerged on to the trail. We had seen no big game, and we were covered with swamp mud, and further ornamented with white chalk. Then, when we caught up the wagon, Elijah informed us he had passed five splendid elk, close to the road, the largest he ever saw!

But our longings to behold big game were fulfilled that night, though not quite as we expected.

We pitched our tent on the Yellowstone banks, by a lovely bend that carried it through great rocks further down. Behind us were thick forests, and in front long blue lines of hills. It looked a splendid place for trout, with its deep pools and gravelly shallows, so, though it was getting dark, A brought out his rods, and in a very few minutes had secured some fine big fellows, which were delicious, grilled for supper.

The men had stupidly left the axe behind at our lunching place, and so it happened our tent was not very well pegged down that night. However, as it was clear still weather, we thought it did not matter, not dreaming of other alarms. I was rather tired and slept soundly, and it must have been about one o'clock when I was awakened by funny little squeaks near the tent, and I heard the men from the wagon, about ten yards off, calling out and trying to frighten something away. This ceased for a little. Then presently I heard something creeping round the tent, and some more squeals. The lamp was dimly burning, and I turned it on the entrance, which was the unpegged part. Something was squeezing itself under the canvas, something about the size of a badger, black and smooth, and with a sharp little nose. I turned the lamp full upon it, and we stared at each other, both much surprised. My stick was close at hand, so I whacked on the ground, upon which the little beast turned tail in a hurry, and scuttled out as fast as it could. A. by this time was awake, and professed to be much surprised that I, who was so fond of live creatures, should object to the poor little thing. "As if it would have hurt us," he remarked, as he turned over and went to sleep again. However, dearly as I love the animal world, I prefer not to have unknown species thereof rambling about my sleeping apartment, and so I lay awake on the chance of having another visit. Before long I heard something walking about with heavy lumbering gait, some few yards off. Then it came nearer, walked slowly round the tent, sniffing along the bottom, and brushing up against the canvas as it passed. With some difficulty I awoke A.

"There's a wild beast outside!" I cried, "and it's trying to get in—what shall we do!" A. replied that he would rather be eaten than wake up, and that it was most likely a poor little mink or inoffensive creature of that kind, and I had better go to sleep again. But at that moment it began to move once more, there was a shuffling at the entrance—a great big something bulging it out as it tried to poke its way through. Then, as we watched, horrified (having no guns in the tent), we saw a large brown head thrust through the insecurely fastened opening. "It's a wolf!" I shrieked, "and it wants to eat us!" And we seized our sticks and made a terrific noise to frighten the monster. He certainly was surprised, for he quickly withdrew his nose, and we heard him sloping off. I was dying with curiosity to see what he was like, and at last summoned up courage to peep out. It was early morning, and a faint cold light made everything distinctly visible. There, squatting a few yards off, was our visitor, watching us, and trying to make up his mind whether to investigate further. I had no desire for a closer acquaintance with him, however, and beat on the sides of the tent with my stick, and yelled at him in a way that evidently struck terror into his savage breast, for he turned tail and trotted off, and I lost sight of him below the hill. After this we barricaded the entrance and made it as secure as we could, and A. promised to keep watch for the rest of the night. However, I had not the smallest inclination to close an eye even, and as soon as it was light enough we got up and roused the men to prepare breakfast. We found they had had a lively night also, as they had had mink after the fish, and our big brown visitor also, which latter had been attracted by the elk steak. They declared it was a wolverine, which is a very cowardly sort of brute, and rarely shows fight or attacks mankind. But they confided in A. afterwards that it was really a cinnamon bear, but that they did not like to tell me for fear I should be too much alarmed to sleep in the tent again, whereas nobody minded wolverines. However, as I told them, one was quite as alarming to me as the other, though, now it was all over, I was not ill-pleased at having seen one of these interesting beasts so near; for many people go through the Yellowstone without seeing a vestige of a bear, especially if they keep on the trail.

The coyotes and wolves are much scarcer than they were, as the cattlemen have poisoned and killed them in large numbers, owing to their depredations among the young calves, etc. The mountain lion also, a horribly savage beast, something like a small panther, has been trapped and hunted down to a large extent, and is not often seen.

There are several species of bear in the Rockies.[3] But I must not wander off on bear stories. That day we had grand sport—if hauling in fish as fast as you throw the line can be called sport! And indeed, after catching about thirty splendid trout, weighing from one and a half to two pounds apiece, in less than an hour, we felt it was becoming butchery.

We saddled up that afternoon and had a glorious ride of about sixteen miles to the Yellowstone Lake. The trail ran pretty near to the river, which grew gradually wider and wider, broadening out here and there and leaving little islands in the midst. Endless masses of dark forest were on our right, and endless hazy stretches of distant Rockies far over the valley on the other side. Everywhere wild and free, untrodden and untouched!

We made a detour through the woods, thick with fallen pine. As long as there was foot room between the trunks, the horses would walk quite unconcernedly over them, picking their way very cleverly, and making funny little hops over the very big ones.

We reached the Yellowstone Lake in the evening, and camped in a little knoll by its side. The water is of a silvery grey color, clear as crystal, and of enormous depth. It had a peculiar spirit-like aspect. The mountains which

---

3 There are only two species of bear in the park, black bears and grizzly bears. Early tourists thought different colors of black bears (black, brown, and cinnamon) were different species.

surrounded it to the east looked like grey phantoms in the evening light. To the west, great forests cast black shadows, contrasting sharply with the pure snowy peaks behind, while densely wooded islands looked like spots of ink upon its pearly surface.

We followed the same road back for about eleven miles, passing our late camping ground by the river, where we stopped to lunch. On turning into the road that leads to the canyon, we left the trees behind, and passed over undulating ground covered only with the sweet scented but monotonous sagebrush. Now and then we crossed a little creek bridged by round pine logs, placed side by side on trestles without any attempt at making them secure, the consequence being they generally rolled about in a manner not altogether pleasant, and one of the horses' legs was pretty sure to go through as we passed over them.

Before entering Hayden Valley we crossed Sulphur Mountain. This is a great cone-shaped pile of pure sulphur, the color of gamboge, and encrusted with the loveliest yellow crystals. It was very hot,—as we found when we sat down on a crystal ridge to watch a big sulphur pool, which lay in a little dip in the hill, boiling and spluttering forth its yellow streams. At every little crevice steam of a sulfurous odor was puffing forth, and we amused ourselves by making little vent-holes with our sticks to help it to escape.

We soaped that sulphur pool, too, with our very last bars, in the hope it might turn into a geyser. But though at last in desperation we cast in a pound of butter, some cart-grease, and a piece of cheese, not even these dainties had any effect upon it, though it sucked them greedily into its funnel-like throat. All it would do was to send up a little squirt from its center. It seems always to be in a furiously boiling condition, its overflow streaming in numerous little crystallized yellow channels down the hill-side, over which our horses very gingerly picked their way.

A few miles beyond the Sulphur Mountain, we came once more to the Yellowstone River, which here was broad and clear, with peaceful grassy banks. Its bright green waters, though quite unruffled, were flowing very swiftly, however; and then gradually, as the valley begins to contract lower down, they gather themselves together to burst their way through the great jagged rocks which form the entrance to the Canyon.

It was dark by the time we had fixed on our camping-ground above the Upper Falls, the majestic roar of which sounded solemnly in our ears. We waited for the moon to rise, and then set forth to feast our eyes on the great Canyon and the Lower Falls, the highest falls of that volume of water in the world.

We followed a path cut out of the mountainside which leads almost to the top of the Canyon, a pretty steep ascent. Thick trees on either side obscured the view, until presently, following the guide, we crawled along a narrow ridge that stood at right angles from the trail, at the end of which was a pinnacle of rock, where one could cling and look up and down and all around.

We were speechless—thrilled! Beneath us yawned 2,000 feet, black, immeasurable. The moon glinted on innumerable overhanging fragments and columns of rock, some sharp and pointed, like cathedral spires, piercing up from the depths below. Dark pine forests fringed the edges, and here and there, hurled against the rocks in their fearful descent, lay fallen trunks—headlong—stretching forth gaunt arms of horror. Twenty-four miles that awful chasm splits its way through the heart of the mountains. A mighty river is frantically bursting through its far-away depths, so far, no sound of its rushing can ever reach the ear.

And then the Falls! Imagine a vast white gliding mass, a wall of snow, pouring itself between two great shoulders of rock in one splendid plunge into the black abyss, a plunge of nearly 400 feet, amidst wreathing and wafting clouds of spray and wind-flecked foam. It was a sight before which Niagara, Shoshone, all we had ever seen, or dreamed, of sublime and wonderful power and beauty, faded and was lost. Awe-stricken and breathless, how insignificant we felt clinging there!

By daylight it appeared even yet more wonderful because of the entrancing colors of its marvelous setting. For on every side are crags of the most weird and curious forms, sometimes bathed with crimson as with blood; sometimes splashed with shades of orange, or ribbed with yellow and brown. There are rocky ledges smoothly laid with vivid green as with a painter's brush. There are chalky beds of mountain torrents now dry, or glacier-worn channels, trailing in sparkling whiteness to the distant river far below. Across and athwart it all lie black shadows from rugged battlements and towers; riven and torn by a giant power and poised upon the sharp descent. And the eagles hover and circle over the pinnacles and spires, on the points of some of which they have built their nests. And above the falls gleam the rapids, as, lashing themselves against the walls of rock on either side, they madly tear along. And a rainbow ever comes and goes, and irradiates with its bright colors the great white, solemn, plunging mass, and melts into the misty wreaths of foam. And—one feels one will never look upon such a scene again. It is Nature's masterpiece!

The next day we forded the river with some difficulty, about a mile above the Upper Falls, and explored the other side, a thing very few people had ever done, Smithson remarked, which was satisfactory to hear. We tied up the horses and walked for a long way by the broken Canyon side. Its vastness seemed to grow upon one, as we caught glimpses of the river between the jutting crags, diminished so as to appear like a thin blue ribbon fluttering in the breeze. We loosened huge boulders and rolled them over, and watched them crashing down, bounding from rock to rock, till they looked no larger than pebbles and were lost to view. Not the faintest sound of their reaching the bottom could one even hear.

So much time was spent over this fascinating occupation it was quite late when we reached camp. Here we were greeted by Elijah with the displeasing information that the wagon horses had been stolen and not a trace of them was to be found. It was no good doing anything that night, but early the following morning the men, having fortunately secured two mounts from the "hotel," started in pursuit, and guided by the discovery of the tracks made by Billy's off hind foot, which had lost a shoe, they found them at last in a little gully, into which they had been driven, about eight miles distant, and brought them triumphantly home.

About twelve o'clock that day we started for Norris Basin, fifteen miles distant. We followed the edge of the Canyon for some way, up and down, between rocks and trees, such awful dizzy heights, I fain dismounted and led the callous Snip, heedless of A. who remarked that I was much safer on his legs than my own. Then we turned off and took a short cut over some wild stretches of valley and forest.

As we were "loping" the horses across one of the grassy slopes, Smithson, who was in front, cried out suddenly, "Four bears, as I'm alive—if that ain't derned luck!" And sure enough, there, about a hundred yards in front of us, were four big brown lumpy-looking things, watering at a little stream that flowed at the foot of the tree-covered hills. We were so excited, we cast prudence to the winds and galloped straight for them, leaping the brooks that crossed our path, and coming right upon them as they were ponderously making their way back to the woods. The horses were rather frightened, though not as much as one would have expected, and we succeeded with some difficulty in keeping them up to our "big game." The four great beasts turned round and eyed us solemnly for a few moments, then snuffing the air disdainfully, as if we were beneath contempt, slowly shuffled off. We followed them a little way, until they disappeared among the trees, but they did not hurry their pace. It certainly was a very thrilling sight, and we heard afterwards that to see so many full-grown bears together was most unusual. I suppose if we had in any way molested them, our lives, even on horseback, would hardly have been worth a moment's purchase; but we only wanted to look, and so we were safe!

We turned on to the trail about eight miles from Norris Basin, a broad, graded, road, which made us feel within reach of civilized regions once more, and consequently rather damped our spirits. It led gently downhill through an endless forest of bastard fir, or bull pine as they are called, their slender upright stems packed so thickly together only a small beast could have squeezed itself amongst them.[4] We entered another beautiful canyon as we approached Norris Basin, with huge perpendicular cliffs and the Gibbon River dashing turbulently close to the roadside. The cascades here are very lovely. The water sweeps down a gentle incline of about eighty feet of moss-covered rock, spreading itself out like a sheet of frosted silver. Leaving this behind, we soon entered, descending still, upon the Norris Basin, and from the curling wreaths of vapor arising from white barren patches amongst the trees, we could see we were in Geyserland once more.

We camped near a winding stream, cool and clear, across the Norris fork of the Gibbon River, and were much disturbed all night by the horses belonging to some other camping party, who seemed to mistake our tent for that of their owners, and came trampling and whinnying round, evidently wanting to be fed. Smithson, who spent most of his night trying to induce them to roam elsewhere, "guessed t'other folks were short of corn, and had driv 'em over river to us"—which seemed to us very reprehensible conduct.

There is a neat little stage house at Norris Basin, where we procured some fresh milk, a great luxury; and having had an icy cold bath in the stream (making S. and E. "chatter all over to see us"), we sallied forth to explore the

4 Georgina is describing the Lodge Pole Pine, a common species in this area of the park.

Norris Geyser. The road led through the barren formation where they chiefly lie, some extinct, some just bursting into life, others dying away. The "Constant" was sending up energetic spouts, and the "Minute Man" showered a lovely fountain regularly as its name denotes. From a black-looking hole on the side of a mound a volume of steam bursts forth every few seconds with such a blast, it is as the roar of countless engines letting off steam together. Then there was a furiously boiling mud-pot, sending up tongues of liquid, pale drab mud, writhing and twisting as if it were some tortured spirit. Hot and cool pools lay close together. The Emerald Pool was like a fairy's grotto, liner with lovely coral-like forms, and tinted with the most exquisite emerald hues.

We were very anxious to see the "Monarch" display, as it is the largest in these regions, and owing to the shape of its orifice it goes up in a long thin sheet unlike any other. It lies in a hollow scooped out of the hillside, shaped like a sort of throne, and is supposed to play every twenty-four hours. We determined to see it, even if we waited all day, and seated ourselves to watch, sending Smithson back for our lunch. I believe after an hour or so of expectation we had a nap, not having enjoyed very excellent repose by night.

They had hardly gone five minutes when the "Monarch" began to bestir itself, and we retired to a safe distance.[5] It boiled up, slopped over several times, and the most uncanny noise proceeded from its long thin mouth. Then it burst forth, up and up, widening and spreading, soaring higher and higher—like glistening icebergs endowed with life—like snowy mountains leaping into being. The sun was shining from behind and turned it as it fell into showers of glory, and the whole sky was obscured by the clouds of spray. It played for nearly an hour, pouring forth a river of water; then it lowered its crest and dwindled into intermittent and attenuated forms, like white ghosts trying to escape and ever falling down. Then, at last, with a sobbing noise it sank to rest and peace.

Though the "Monarch" is not so high as the "Beehive," or even "Old Faithful," it is of much greater width and volume of water; indeed, we considered it quite the most beautiful geyser we had seen—the last and the best.

From Norris Basin to Mammoth Hot Springs is about twenty-one miles. Until lately the trail led over a. very steep mountain 3,000 feet high,

---

5 Monarch Geyser has been dormant since 1913.

but now the Government Engineers have constructed a new road through the Canyon of the Gardiner, making it quite an easy journey.

We made very good time the first seven miles after leaving the Basin, crossing by a gently sloping pass, the divide which separates the waters of the Gardiner River from the Gibbon. A lovely sheet of water spread before us as we left the pass, and extended for more than a mile along the side of the road. Beaver Lake it is called, as it was formed by dams constructed across the Green River by these clever little beasts. Among the grass-covered ridges, and along the swampy edges of the lake, wild geese and crane were splashing, while ducks and waterfowl innumerable were basking upon its serene surface.

Rising from the eastern shore of Beaver Lake are the Obsidian Cliffs, "unequalled in the world," as the guidebooks say. They certainly are very curious, these walls of black and violet glass, bright and glistening, and streaked here and there with red and yellow. To make a road through this barrier was a great difficulty. It was only accomplished by lighting fires upon the huge masses of glass which blocked the way, and then when these had sufficiently expanded with the heat, cold water was poured upon them, causing them to fracture into fragments. This obsidian is a species of lava, and is extremely difficult to cut. It was much valued by the Indians for arrowheads and tools, specimens of which are still picked up.

As we entered Mammoth Springs we perceived with some revulsion that we were indeed in the gay world once more. Smartly attired ladies were strolling about, and we passed a group of young men in tennis flannels, with rackets in their hands. It nearly took our breath away when we rode up to the hotel, and saw at what a palatial building we were to be "located." There was an imposing facade of about four hundred feet, with a broad terrace, where beauty and fashion were disporting themselves in all their glory. I descended from dear Snip's back under their astonished glances, and for one weak moment almost wished my attire was more feminine, and my buckskin leggings not tied up with pieces of string where the buttons had come off.

We had quite a business getting our kit together, as it had got rather mixed up with the hay which had burst out of our mattresses. However, we were clear at last, said good-bye to our faithful steeds, and watched them, and our outfit, wend their way to the camping ground where they were to pass the night before starting on their return journey.

101

We were supplied with a huge bedroom, fitted with electric light, and with such spacious wardrobes we quite wished we had some clothes to put in them. The hotel holds three hundred "guests," and it seemed pretty full. The people were very amusing to watch, they were such a funny mixture. Officers in uniform, from the depot, looking very immaculate; business men taking their holiday in black coats and top hats; cowboys and stage-drivers dropping in for a dinner and a wash after "rounding up"; and every description of tourist and traveller, in every sort of "get up" imaginable. The women were most of them very smart, some with low dresses, and flowers in their hair. These, however, we heard, were not "transients" (the American term for the sojourner of a day or two), but were boarding there for the summer.

The manager was very civil, and took us into his private office for conversation, and blew up the manager of the Canyon "Hotel" by telephone, on our complaining of his refusal to sell us some salt because we were "campers out" and brought him no profit.[6]

Next morning, having paid into Smithson's hands the money for our outfit, which he was to take back to Beaver Canyon, and said good-bye to him and Elijah with violent hand-shakings and complimentary speeches all round, we started to explore the springs. These lie in about four hundred acres of white travertine formation, much the same as in the geyser regions, but the springs themselves are quite different. At first sight they look like lovely marble terraces one above the other, rounded and escalloped. But on approaching them one discovers that they are formed by clusters of little basins full of hot water, each ornamented with a delicately molded rim, and with curved and fluted sides. The water trickles over the edges from one to another, blending them together with the effect of a frozen waterfall. One can walk up between the terraces, where the water no longer flows and the formations are crumbling to decay, and admire the lovely coloring with which some of the basins are coated; cream and salmon, green and yellow. The Minerva terrace is one of the most perfect of these; it is fed by a powerful spring laden with oxides, with which it paints the walls of its basin in richly shaded colors of cream, pink and copper.[7] But the most beautiful of all are those that are pure

---

6 Complaints against concessionaires for refusing service to tourists who provided their own transportation and shelter, who were derisively called "Sagebrushers," were common at this time.

7 The differing colors in Yellowstone hot springs are due primarily to differing microorganisms that thrive in different water temperatures.

white; some of which are called the Pulpit terraces. No human architect ever designed such delicate flutings and such intricate moldings as adorn these wonderful formations. But they glisten coldly in their spotless whiteness, for they are dead, and the waters that built them up have gone elsewhere, and left them to a gradual, though as yet far-distant, decay. There is hope for them still, however, they may live again; fresh springs may break out, and with their deposits build up what is crumbling away. If not, they will someday be like the many terraces higher up the hill, that have quite lost their lovely forms, and in the earth-filled basins of which dwarf pine and cedar have taken root, and grown, and flourished.

The chief spring is the "Cleopatra," which lies in a mound of deposit about forty feet high. Down its sides, where the water overflows, are numerous smaller basins, fringed with pure white stalactites. Some of the cones are very curious. There is one that points up like a sort of finger; it is forty-seven feet high, and it took fifty-four centuries to grow. They seem to increase at the rate of about a foot a century, so one can judge their age pretty accurately. We saw several infant cones only two or three centuries old; others that must have been growing for thousands of years.

There are all sorts of surprises—pits, grottoes, and caverns—as one explores further up amongst the ridges and hollows and white ghostly-looking rocks. There is the Stygian Cave, the mouth of which is covered with the corpses of insects and birds caught and killed by the poisonous vapor whilst flying over; and further on is the deadly River Styx, with expiring creatures fluttering on its banks. There is another cave with dark mysterious chambers, and the Boiling River flowing underneath; and beyond, a narrow fissure, where you hear its waters pouring through a bed of sulphur and arsenic with a hissing, grating noise. It would take weeks to exhaust the wonders of these Mammoth Springs.

We had heard a rumor that there was a hot lake where we could have a swim, and so had brought our bathing dresses with us. After much searching we found it at last, lying in a hollow surrounded on one side with bushes and stunted trees. We entered with some caution, not wishing to be boiled alive, but soon discovered where its spring lay and kept at a comfortable distance, where we could just bear ourselves, taking refuge along the more tepid edges when we got too hot. It was altogether great fun; though the air felt dreadfully cold when we came out, and we were quite glad to hurry home to lunch.

As we were discussing this said meal, I began to extol the delights of our bath to our table companions, but my remarks were received rather coldly, and I noticed the horrified glances cast upon me by some ladies opposite. Having terribly shocked the modest Mormons by bathing in Salt Lake with bare arms and without stockings, I thought my attire had something to say to it—perhaps I had been seen by one of them. But as I was looking through the local guide book I learnt the awful act I had committed, as after describing Bath Lake and expatiating upon its charms, it remarks with much pathos, "Ladies, alas, cannot even see it, owing to the male bathers that occupy it exclusively." By the time I had discovered this, however, our audience had vanished, so I could not retrieve my character by explaining that not a vestige of any sort of bather did we set eyes upon.

After lunch we walked down the valley to the Gardiner River, where it flows side by side with the Boiling River, the latter joining it further on. It is here that one can catch one's trout and cook him without changing one's position—standing on the bank between the two streams and popping the fish caught in the Gardiner into the hot river the other side, where he is done to a turn in about five minutes! We should like to have tried this for ourselves, but the Gardiner had been overfished that season, and we had not a chance.[8]

The next morning we started by stage for Cinnabar, about six miles distant, to which place the Northern Pacific runs its branch line from Livingstone.[9] The road passes through the Gardiner Canyon and is flanked with magnificent cliffs and pinnacles of rock on either side. In the distance is Sentinel Peak, with its humanlike face uplifted, staring into the heavens; and Mount Everts, which is always capped with snow. Then through Gardiner City; the city consisting of a dozen or so wooden shanties and log-houses, chiefly burnt down, as they had had a fire the night before, and the belongings of the inhabitants were strewed about all over the road. We nearly ran over a billiard table, and just escaped a serious accident over some pots and pans.

The train was waiting for us at Cinnabar and took us through the Lower Canyon, where we had a grand view of the Rockies, with Emigrant Peak

8 Cooking fish in hot springs without removing them from the line is possible in several places in the park. The most famous is the Fishing Cone on the edge of Lake Yellowstone.

9 The railroad didn't reach the northern entrance to Yellowstone Park at Gardiner, Montana, until 1903.

13,000 feet high, the somber gulches of which are rich in gold; and passing the Devil's Slides—long crimson-stained courses, formed ages ago by streams of lava pouring down from the heights above. Glaciers have stranded gigantic boulders between the slopes, some of which, wind and water worn, take curious and fantastic forms like unto beasts and birds and living things.

We had to wait several hours at Livingstone to be taken up by the mail from San Francisco, and employed our time in searching for a buffalo robe among the hunter's stores, for which the place is renowned. We secured the only one we could find, for sixty dollars, a handsome hide, though only that of a cow (a bull's, we were told, would cost over a hundred dollars). A few years ago we could have picked up either for four or five dollars, but so successfully has the buffalo been shot down and slaughtered, that it is well nigh exterminated; it is said, indeed, that there are hardly 300 head left in the whole of the States.

It has been estimated that as many as four and a half million were killed between 1872 and 1874 alone. The skin hunters used to start out in parties with a regular outfit of wagon, tent, cook, etc. When they got near a herd they would encamp and prepare for the slaughter. One hunter was sufficient, the rest being skinners, as the only important point was to get to leeward of the herd and to keep well hidden from view; for this exceedingly stupid beast, as long as he smelt or saw nothing, would appear quite callous to noise, and would go on browsing contentedly with his brethren falling dead around him, displaying only a mild curiosity at their death struggles. Thus very often as many as fifty or sixty beasts would be shot down without a change of position. The bodies were usually left to the vultures and coyotes, only the skins being secured. Their bones, that used to whiten the prairie, have been now collected and sent off for manufacture into buttons and various other things. In Canada, as skin-hunting is prohibited, there are a few hundred head still left, but even these mysteriously dwindle, as do those within the Reservations in the States, and soon the buffalo—as well as the Indian—will have succumbed to the advance of the civilized (?) world; and cowboys and horses, cattle ranches and beer saloons, will occupy the vast ranges where both once used to roam.

As we were sauntering about after our purchase, we were invited, by the owner of another hunter's store close by, to come and see a mountain lion, the only one, he asserted, that had ever been tamed. It was in a little back room, chained to a strong iron staple in the floor, around which it was pacing, uttering low growls. It appeared very like a small panther, and seemed anything but "tame," snarling at us as if longing to spring. It was in awe of its master, however, and cowered down each time he cracked his whip. He made it do several tricks with a dear retriever dog, who did not seem half to like it. "Come and kiss Miss Pussy," said the man, and the dog went up to it and laying his paw across its neck licked its face. He then put a piece of meat on its nose, and told the dog to come and fetch it away. "He doesn't care for this part," remarked the man; "she's had him by the throat once or twice." However, this time Miss Pussy allowed her dinner to be abstracted with only a snarl of disapprobation. "I wouldn't take a thousand dollars for her," continued Miss Pussy's master, with great pride. "Barnum'd give his eyes to have her! Just look at her iron paws, one blow 'ud lie you dead as mutton—what, you brute—you would, would you!" (Miss Pussy tries to gnaw his boot but is lashed off.) "Yes, I take her out walking in the mountains sometimes, and with her chain off, when we are out of the town; only I take precious good care I follow her, not she me," he added, with a laugh.

In spite of these attractive traits, we were not sorry to say good-bye to Miss Pussy, as we heard the sound of our approaching train, and hurried off to secure a "stateroom" to ourselves, as we had a journey of two days and nights before reaching Chicago.

American traveling is, certainly, very comfortable and well arranged. Our stateroom, with a lavatory and hot water, was upholstered in terra-cotta plush, was lighted by electric light, and could be warmed, if necessary, by hot pipes. Our beds had spring mattresses, and we had an attendant ever ready to bring us iced water, books from the library, fruit, or anything we desired. Excellent meals were served in the dining-car (on some lines they give you a hot bath), and one could get plenty of exercise by walking through the cars, all of which were connected by little bridges. However, in spite of all these luxuries, we gazed sadly and regretfully on the fading-away peaks of the wonderland in which we had passed so exceedingly delightful a time, feeling that never, wherever we might go, should we behold so many marvels, or such grand and beautiful sights; never should we feel within us such an exhilaration of health and strength, such a capacity for enjoyment, as in this entrancing Yellowstone region.

Western Girls Don't Need Chaperones

Alice Richards—1898

Alice Richards was the daughter of Wyoming's fourth governor, William A. Richards. In 1898, S. S. Huntley, general manager of the Yellowstone National Park Transportation Company, invited Alice to tour the park as his guest. Of course, that meant she got a first-class tour in a comfortable coach driven by a knowledgeable guide. She stayed in company hotels that rivaled the best in the nation at her own expense.

Alice eagerly organized a party with three other young women, but she couldn't find an older person to serve as their chaperone. Undaunted, she and her companions decided to take the trip without an escort. They feared they would be considered uncultured "western girls," so they resolved to be on their best behavior.

Alice's father arranged for railroad passes and the party traveled to the park from Cheyenne by a circuitous route. In her reminiscence, Alice describes the places she stayed, the sights she saw, and the people she met—especially the young men. She interspersed her account with notes from her trip diary.

This version of Alice's story is from the Burlingame Collection at the Montana State University Library.

* * * *

December 1897 and January 1898 had been spent in Washington D.C. as the guest of Senator and Mrs. Warren. Among the callers at the Senator's was S.S. Huntley, General Manager of the Yellowstone National Park Transportation Company, headquarters at the Mammoth Hot Springs in the park.

My father and mother, Senator and Mrs. D.C. Clark and Mr. and Mrs. W.R. Schnitter had made a tour of the park the preceding summer. Mr. Huntley said that not enough people from Wyoming were visiting the park and said if I would get up a party he would provide transportation through the park. I was greatly interested and began to talk about such a trip as soon

When Wyoming governor's daughter Alice Richards visited the park as the guest of the Yellowstone Park Transportation Company in 1898, she received comfortable accommodations at hotels like the Cottage at Mammoth Hot Springs.
AUTHOR'S COLLECTION.

as I reached home. I had expected to find it easy to get older friends to join me, but no one was interested though the expense at hotels we knew was not very high. When I was about to give up on the idea my father said he wanted my sister Ruth and myself to go. He spoke to Jesse Knight, the Judge of the State Supreme Court who said his daughter Harriet could go. She found that a university friend of hers, Harriet Fox, would like to make the trip—so the plans were made and we four left Cheyenne on July 30, via the Cheyenne and Northern Railroad.

All the details of the trip were in my hands—I was the "Miss Manager" or big boss. I knew Hattie Knight slightly, Hattie Fox not at all, but we got along splendidly together. Not once on the trip did they trouble me with suggestions or remarks; they let me lead and did what seemed best. They were certainly fine companions.

In those good old days it was not hard to get passes on the railroads and my father procured passes for all of us on the necessary lines. I also had a Western Union Telegraph frank. Being very conscientious I used the latter only when necessary.

Our trip was north to Orin Junction on the "Cheyenne and Northern" (a train not noted for its speed) then east to Crawford, Nebraska, onto the Chicago and Northwestern and northwest from Crawford on the Chicago, Burlington and Quincy. We reached Crawford at ten o'clock, got up at 4:30 so as to be sure to get the train at 5:35. As manager I was anxious that we should be ready on time—a trait I fear I have never outgrown. We were a hungry group when we reached Edgemont, South Dakota, for breakfast. We reached Livingstone, Montana, in time for the evening meal and stayed all night at a hotel, entering the park the next day, August 1, 1898.

Prices are interesting. Lodging for Ruth and me at Crawford was 50 cents each. As I remember it we four had one large room with two double beds. Breakfast at the Edgemont was 75 cents apiece; lodging and breakfast at Livingstone was the same. Good lodging and good food!

We had a gay time on the trip to Orin because we were allowed the freedom of the train and rode on the engine, on the rear platform, and in the baggage car. I think Hattie Fox knew the engineer—that is not in my notes. We met several people whom we knew and had a generally good time—but we always remembered we were "ladies." I was 21 and a half years old; the Hatties were a little younger and Ruth was 15. We three older girls were probably somewhat mature and used to taking care of ourselves. I had been with my father since January 1895 and the Hatties were either juniors or seniors at the State University. Ruth was tall for her age and mingled well with us older girls. More of the impression we four "girls all alone" made during the park trips.

Should have stated above that from Livingston, which is on the main line of the Northern Pacific Railroad, we took a branch of said line, which runs 51 miles south to the town of Cinnabar, Montana, which is the northern entrance to the park. Here we were met by park employees who took charge of us. "Tourists are conveyed in six-horse tally-ho coaches to the Mammoth Hot Springs Hotel, seven miles from Cinnabar."

The other tourists were "conveyed" by stagecoach, but the four of us were taken in charge by, . . . put in the park wagon with two seats behind the driver.

Four schoolteachers from Brooklyn wanted a wagon also. They didn't like the coach. "We can't climb on the top of that thing. We do not see why those giddy girls have a wagon when we can't have one." So, right there, easterners began to be critical of "those western girls." Maybe here is the place to say that they finally changed their minds. Even the teachers said they wished eastern girls had the high spirits and courtesy of us giddy western girls. We were full of fun, but we were always polite and courteous to others and didn't do anything out of the way. However, after we had been on the way a day or two, Mrs. Meyer from Red Lodge, Montana, suggested to me that some of us ride in their somewhat larger wagon. She said, "You do not need chaperones as you behave well, but those easterners do not understand our ways and will take away a better report if you seem to be of our party." Being loyal westerners we agreed—I remember I was very glad for I did feel the responsibility of my party.

At Cinnabar we were approached by an emissary from Mr. Huntley who ushered us over to the park wagon mentioned above. The baggage was with us and we started out with Mr. Murphy as driver to get our first view of

Four-horse stagecoaches sped tourists like Alice Richards and her friends across the many miles between sights. Buses took over in 1916.
NATIONAL PARK SERVICE.

Wonderland ahead. In a note to me, Mr. Huntley had said that he would try to find an honest driver for us, but quite soon Mr. Murphy began telling quite tall tales of the rather rough country through which we were passing. We didn't "ah" and "oh" quite enough to suit him and pretty soon he turned to us and said, "Just where are you girls from?" We tried to say we were tenderfeet—but it didn't suit him. When he found that the Hatties were from the University and Ruth and I from Cheyenne, he was quite abashed. "Why didn't Mr. Huntley tell me I was driving western girls? I thought I was going to have some nice innocent girls from the east."

Later he said, "I was taking someone else's place today but I am going to ask Mr. Huntley to let me take you all the way through the park—even though I can't tell my tall tales." We assured him we would gladly listen and would be glad to have him for all the trip—which we did and found him a very good driver and a kind friend.

The first stop on the trip after leaving the railroad is the Mammoth Hot Springs—which fully lived up to their name. However, this is not a tale of the park, but of four girls who managed their own trip—with the help of park employees. The people were the greatest item of interest. There were many easterners, and others from many parts of the country.

One person was Arthur Morse. He was from New York City and had enlisted in the regular army hoping to be sent to Cuba or the Philippines, where he would have real adventures. Instead he was sent out as a U.S. Guide in the park. He guided us around "Hells Half Acre" and told us his troubles. He was tall, good looking, very courteous and quite won our sympathy. That evening at the Fountain Hotel all gathered for a pleasant evening and we hoped to see Arthur—but he did not appear. Other guides were there from places nearby and we girls were very much sought after—but we missed Arthur. He either was jealous of the other guides who were largely from the University of Minnesota—or he felt that as a good army man he shouldn't be associated with them.

We were about ready to break up the party when someone came in with the news that the "Great Fountain" geyser would be in eruption in about an hour. There are certain indications which make it possible to foretell the time of the going up of this seldom seen geyser. We were naturally eager to see it—but it was about two miles away, with no conveyances available. We three older girls started bravely out—leaving Ruth at the hotel.

111

Notes from diary: At the Fountain Hotel we were assigned to nice rooms where we bathed and dressed for dinner. Hattie Fox's face quite burned. Early evening tour the section nearby with Mr. Butler, Transportation Agent. (Had met him at Mammoth), also Lt. Arnold, Mr. Higgins and Mr. Summers. "Little Recruit" didn't appear. Great Fountain later. Party: H. Knight and guide. Mr. and Mrs. Arford, Mr. Hubbard and Mr. Burt walked. I went to pasture on horseback with Mr. McMullan. On return found rest had gone on. Caught up with them. H. Fox and Mr. Higgins walked. Mr. Summers rode with us. Got there just in time. Great Fountain played 45 minutes, lighted by a fine moon.

Hattie Fox and Mr. Higgins rode back—two horses.

A.R. and Ra McMillan rode "double deck"—slow white horse.

H.K and Mr. Sommers walked. "We" to pasture again. Raided kitchen. Crackers and milk. Bed at three—up at six.

Again from diary: West Thumb. We to the lake were we had a fine trip on the boat, our party gathered in stern. Stopped at Dot Island, saw buffalo and mountain sheep. Mrs. Meyers a fine chaperone.

"Lake Hotel. There at four o'clock. Had a large room with four windows facing the lake. Lakeside promenade. Rested and slept an hour. All had boat rides. In even H. Fox ride with Mr. Burgie. Watched moon rise. Fine time had by all. Easterners still jealous of western girls, but we knew we were behaving and didn't mind them—laughed at them. We did have good time and probably were a little too unreserved for those from the east, esp. Boston and Brooklyn."

The next day we went on to the Canyon Hotel. There had been rain the day before and it continued until about 2:30 of the day. We had been offered horses for a ride and went in spite of rain, Mr. Murphy as guide. Mr. Hubbard from Wheeling, West Virginia, accompanied us. Mr. Hubbard is a large man and had done little riding. "Wondered if his horse could carry him." We rode to Point Lookout, Grand View, and Inspiration Point—marvelous views of the canyon from all points. "Too magnificent for words." "Passed the doctors in the surrey." Presume this meant the four teachers from Brooklyn. Perhaps they were happy to have a ride in the surrey instead of the coach. Mr. Hubbard wished that eastern girls had so much of our spirit. When we returned daughters were interested only in boys and fancy work. When we returned to the hotel the bellboy said we had had the best horses from the hotel stables.

Some of the pictures accompanying this were taken at the Canyon Hotel by Mrs. Ostrander—a tourist. Said she wanted pictures of the girls who were making something of themselves. The Hatties had never been used to horseback riding, but they were game and in spite of lame muscles, went on the trip to Mount Washburn the following day. The party was composed of us four, Mr. Hubbard and guides Murphy and McBride.

Mount Washburn is reached from the Canyon Hotel. It is about ten miles from the Hotel to the summit, from which a grand view is seen, including a glimpse of the Grand Teton in the country to the south. This trip is not always taken by tourists, but to us it was the highlight of the trip. The two Hatties got along very well because at no time did the horses go out of a walk. Ruth and I were experienced riders so enjoyed it hugely. Ruth, unfortunately, wore a round cap that sat on the back of her head instead of the hats we wore. Her nose got very badly sunburned and she had much trouble with it the rest of the trip.

Should not leave this part of the trip without mentioning the "Economic" geyser, or "Little Faithful." It is the joker of the trip. It erupts about every six minutes, the water going to a height of about twenty then falling straight back in without losing any water. In accordance to custom, the guides have the tourists gather closely round the crater, then get a great laugh when the startled folk jump away as the geyser goes up. One of the guides took our pictures before and after—one of which was in the folder put out by the Northwestern Railroad the next year. (These seem to be lost, too bad.)

Although we were from Wyoming we did not have very good outing costumes as we older girls wore long skirts and shirtwaists, my skirt being a black moiré silk, long and fairly full. (It didn't wrinkle or soil). We three had jackets; Ruth had a jacket suit, naturally shorter because of her age. I wore a sailor hat, straw, the other two wore cowboy hats and Ruth wore a cap. We must have had a change of clothes for the evenings but I do not remember what we had. One young man whom we met said, "Why weren't we told that there were parties in the evenings? Here you girls are all dressed up and I have only knickers."

Maybe there should be a word about the members of the male sex whom we met on the trip. Mr. and Mrs. Meyer were chaperoning a Miss Diedrick, who was with us most of the time. (She wore a very sensible outing suit, with a short skirt, as did Mrs. Meyer). The five of us young girls naturally attracted a good deal of attention from the various young men stationed in the park in various capacities—soldiers at Fort Yellowstone, clerks at the hotels, guides at various stops and even some members of the party going through. McKinstry Burt from Detroit was among the latter and was very nice to all of us. We called him the "Brotherly Young Man." The nicest evening was at the Fountain Hotel because Army officers, guides and clerks came from various other places to dance. Imagine the soldiers had to leave early because when we went out to see the Great Fountain they did not go along. All these young men were very nice to us and we probably were a bright spot in a rather humdrum life.

On August 8 we were again at the railroad and starting home. On the way, however, we made a couple of stops. The first was at the Crow Indian Reservation where E. T. Becker was agent. Mr. Becker, his wife and son took us out to the reservation where we saw Indians at home. One recollection is of an Indian girl who impressed me being one of the most beautiful girls I had ever seen.

From the Agency we went on east to Cambria to see the coalmines. We were guests of W.H. Kilpatrick, the mine superintendent and made a trip into the mine—which was very interesting.

And finally we were home again after a trip that will always remain in our memories.

Everything went smoothly, we all behaved as well as if we had been chaperoned—perhaps better. The first few days the other tourists were inclined to be critical, but when they could find nothing to really criticize they one and all decided that western girls were pretty nice people after all.

That was in 1898, when the world had not begun to think that women really mattered, that they really had rights. We have gone a long way since then but I imagine that if a similar group made a similar trip nowadays—and expected courteous treatment as we did—that the group would be treated as well as we were. It is all right to feel that women are the equals of men—but after all, women like men to be courteous and men like to treat women with respect—and that is as it should be. Women are not "just like men" and never will be and it will be a sad day when men forget to be courteous and gentlemanly.

A Mother Takes Her
Seven Children to the Park

Eleanor Corthell—1903

Eleanor Corthell's husband "could only fizz and fume" when she announced in 1903 that she was taking their seven children to Yellowstone National Park by team and wagon. But he couldn't stop her.

By then the park had been transformed from a forbidding wilderness into a genteel resort where an unaccompanied woman could travel without fear of being attacked by Indians or bears. The Army Corps of Engineers, under the direction of Captain Hiram Chittenden, had completed a network of roads in the park that were among the best in the United States, certainly good enough to be navigated by Mrs. Corthell's sixteen-year-old son. There also were stores where the Corthells could buy supplies and post offices where they could keep in contact with family and friends.

Although the park had several grand hotels, the Corthells camped out for their entire two-month adventure. This meant that Mrs. Corthell had to manage not only the logistics of the trip, but also cooking and laundry—all out of doors. That might sound like an enormous challenge, but as Eleanor probably would have pointed out, she would have been in charge of all those duties had she stayed at home.

Employees of park concessionaires couldn't make money off of tourists like the Corthells who provided their own tents, transportation, and food, and derisively referred to them as "Sagebrushers." The term came from the fact that commercial interest claimed the prime camping spots so sagebrushers were forced to camp on sagebrush flats.

Despite the relative tranquility of Yellowstone Park at the time, the Corthells had plenty of adventures. Their travels across the ranch country of central Wyoming reminded them of Owen Wister's novel, The Virginian, *which many consider to be the first Western. In the park they kept their eyes out for black bear cubs like Johnny*

Bear and a grizzly like Wahb, who were the subjects of famous stories by the hugely popular naturalist and writer Ernest Thompson Seton.

Eleanor received a telegram at the Yellowstone Canyon saying her husband would meet the family when they arrived at Mammoth Hot Springs. When they met, Eleanor ceded leadership to him although she had proven herself up to the challenges of crossing Wyoming from corner to corner.

Nellis soon ran afoul of regulations that were enforced by the Army, which ran the park then. But Nellis was a prominent Wyoming attorney and he managed to talk himself down to a two-dollar fine.

Eleanor's story of her family trek was published in June of 1905 in the magazine Independent. *She published an extended version in book form in 1928. The story here draws from both sources.*

* * * *

Nearly half a lifetime I have lived in Laramie, with all the while a great longing to see the wonders of the Yellowstone in season, out of season, when the house was full of babies, even when it was full of measles. As the older children outgrew marbles and dolls, I conceived the bold idea of stowing them all in a prairie schooner and sailing away over the Rocky Mountains, deserts, forests and fords to the enchanted land five hundred miles away.

My husband offered strenuous objection of course to the crazy project, but could only fizz and fume and furnish the wherewithal, for the reasons advanced he found irresistible; such an ideal vacation for the children—a summer out-of-doors, seeing their native state! A chance for their geography, botany, zoology to be naturalized. To be drivers and cooks would put them on their own resources somewhat, a valuable education in itself. So economical, too! Such a fine opportunity for stretching of legs and lungs, with the park at the end! Reasons to turn a man's head you see, so when the boys wrote along the wagon top "Park or Bust" that settled it and we started July 4th, 1903.

I had resolved to "go light." A two seated spring wagon, tent, stove, bedding, clothing, two weeks' provisions, besides my live freight, made up the load behind a pair of big road horses.

The first day out was glorious. We drove thirty-three miles to the steel bridge down the Laramie River. The bracing air, fresh from Snowy Range, the changing scene, the fragrance of prairie flowers and wild sage, the blue

When Eleanor Corthell visited the park in 1903, she worried about her seven children frolicking at the geothermal features like these women at Great Fountain Geyser.
NATIONAL PARK SERVICE.

of lupine and larkspur giving the effect of lakes here and there, the peaceful herds in grass knee deep, created a charm which we accepted as a good omen of the unknown before us.

We camped without tent or stove that night, for the small boys were "heap big Injuns," who scorned civilized ways. They whooped along on the warpath, examined old trails, read the sky, sent the "stinging fatal arrow" after rabbits, clamored for pioneer tales, then rolled up in blankets around the camp fire with only the stars overhead.

During the night we had an amusing experience to scare a tenderfoot blue. Sometime after midnight when the moon rose, I awoke, amazed to see a hundred head of range cattle lined up around us in a semi-circle, still as mice, their great eyes bulging with curiosity. I called to the boys, several heads bobbed up, and away the cattle scampered, only to return again and again in wild-eyed astonishment until their curiosity was sated, when they grazed off. After that I tried to sleep with one eye open. It can't be done out camping.

Early tourists couldn't resist the opportunity to do their laundry in the abundant hot water provided by Yellowstone springs.
NATIONAL PARK SERVICE.

Why does the morning sun inspire one with the fine courage lacking in the pale moonlight? Now I'm brave enough to "shoo" a whole herd of Texas steers or to grapple with all the dragons kind friends conjured for me—treacherous fords, snakes, bad lands—all of them, each and every.

You are wondering how eight people can be comfortable in two seats? That's easy. We piled our bedding fore, aft and amidships, with clothing in pillowslips, so had seats for all, even choice ones. If you were a small boy, for instance, you could sit on a roll of bedding or sack of grain, hang your bare feet over the dash board and hold the whip, if very good, the lines, or you could perch behind ready to hop off to chase a rabbit, or curl up on a soft pile, lay your head in mother's lap and sleep away the drowsy afternoon.

To the bridge there is one road only, beyond the bridge there are a dozen. Which one led to Little Medicine Crossing, our most direct route to Shirley Basin? We didn't know, and couldn't find out for one may travel a whole day beyond the bridge and not meet a soul, so we took the wrong road and had to make a dry camp at Como, reaching Medicine Bow the third day at noon. From here we drove north among the Freezeout Hills, through which "The Virginian" piloted Owen Wister on his way to the Goose Egg Ranch. We arrived at the old Trading place about four o'clock. This is one of famed historic spots in Wyoming, and many thrilling events have occurred here, but now it is abandoned, save that it is occupied by three young freighters passing through.

They courteously offered to camp outside and give us house, but we were afraid of strangers, so after a hasty supper moved on ten miles and spread our tarpaulins on the bare plain.

Arriving at my friend Kirk Dyer's the next morning I told him of my foolish fears that the young men having their horses might have designs on ours, etc. He rebuked sternly and read me such a lecture as I shall never forget.

"Country people are honest," said he, "and you must take it for granted you are safer here than in Laramie and you get a square deal everywhere. Trust people and don't be that suspicions."

Such a happy day the children spent riding horseback eating Mrs. Dyer's cream biscuits.

Adjoining this ranch are the fossil fields of the Freezeout Hills in which two university boys were working. I would have taken them for young Comanches from their yells at sight of home folks.

Travel in Yellowstone Park could be very difficult before the army took over administration of the park in 1886 and the Corps of Engineers took over road construction.
NATIONAL PARK SERVICE.

Next day was different. We were driving gaily along through the Quealy Meadow, where suddenly the wagon sank in the mire. While the horses struggled to pull it out, the king bolt snapped, and off they walked with the front wheels. My driver boy quietly stepped over the dashboard and walked off after them, still holding the lines.

For one despairing moment I thought the end of all things had come, when my wagon parted in the middle. Noticing my forlorn face one youngster thought it was time to laugh and exclaimed, "Gee, Mamma! This isn't exciting. The horses should have run away and smashed a few kids." Seeing how much worse things might have been I thanked my lucky stars and took heart again.

Shirley Basin proved to be the land of the Good Samaritan where every ranchman is your friend and neighbor, who pulls you out of the mud, mends your king bolts, agrees with you in politics, praises your husband and treats you to ice cream in the evening, so the accident makes pleasant memory.

Now I must tell my troubles. We had started really on the third of July, run into a snowstorm and returned. But it was clear and warm and bright the next morning, and in our haste to be off we left the pocketbook in my desk. Imagine my predicament—a mother totally unused to business or cares outside her own domain, one hundred and fifty miles from home, with seven children and two horses to provide for, and not a cent of money!

We discovered our loss a few miles out from Laramie, but just then met friends driving in, who promised to have the pocketbook forwarded; and we went serenely on our way into this dilemma. We were put to our wits end to get oats, as yet our only necessity.[1] The driver suggested that we trade off a hammock; Daughter thought we could better spare bacon. It being a hot day, little Tad generously offered his overcoat as a basis of trade. The driver and I went to the store each trying to brace the other. One was to mention bacon, that failing, the other to try hammock. Oh, I know exactly how a tramp feels when he begins asking for cold bites. At the first question, "Have you oats?" we received a "no" almost with relief, for now we needn't show our hands here.

We walked over to a ranchman's house, nerved up to try a bargain, until we saw the man, and the fine style in which he lived. Then we realized it would be like asking the president to swap a sack of oats for a side of bacon. No, we must put dignity into our need, so quaking like two criminals, I asked Mr. Blank for oats and "to send the bill to my husband, please." A fleeting, quizzical flutter of his eyelid brought out the wretched blunder of the pocketbook.

"But, my dear Madam," said he, "you must not be traveling with all those children to care for and no money." Then he brought from his desk a generous sum, saying, "Your husband can send me his check when convenient." My troubles were over, but was ever a deed more chivalrous "in day of old when knights were bold?"

In the Platte we toiled up the endless hills through deep sand. Sometimes it would be so sidling we would take turns with the spade and literally build a stretch of road. Sometimes we would all help push the wagon up a steep pitch for the dear horses were in a sheep eaten country. When the smaller children grew very tired from climbing they took turns driving. The next older ones I partly carried, partly coaxed, until finally we were all up the

---

1 Oats are high-energy food for horses that keep them fit.

last cruel hill. We suffered severely from thirst, for the water jug had bumped out and broken coming down a rough canyon.

Suddenly someone said "tomatoes." Away down beneath the bedding we found them, cool and just to our taste, one quart can, two, then a third. And as Stewart White said of the cool breeze under a fallen tree, "Never have dinners or wines or men or women or talks of books or scenery or sport or the daintiest refinements of man's inventions given me half the luxury I enjoyed from that cup of tomato." To quote him further, "Real luxury cannot be bought, it must be worked for."

But climbing sandy hills is really not trouble when one is desperate for oats. Still it brought home vividly the suffering of the forty-niners, as the want of the pocketbook made me feel the shame of the penniless tramp.

The children are eagerly interested in everything they see, hear or can catch. Tad announces that we have seen eight horned toads, caught five and mailed three to the chum at home.

Query: Where is the medicine that was in those boxes? Well if they spill the tablets they will have to drink sage tea when ill. Marvelous cures of many kinds in bitter sage.

Everybody is growing handy, even expert in camp work. The boys can skin a cottontail or dress a sage hen equal to Kit Carson himself, while Daughter prepares a savory dinner or packs a mess box good enough for an army general.

The immensity of Wyoming begins to dawn on them. They hunt, swim, explore and so learn to enjoy the special individual flavor of each locality. But all grow tired of the limitless sage—one million acres after another. Why do these vast, treeless plains bear one species of wood only and that so abundantly? When all the coal beds are empty and all the oil wells are dry, Wyoming sagebrush may be relied upon to warm and light the world. It makes an ideal campfire and bakes biscuits perfectly.

We are now over two hundred miles from home and approaching the Beaver Hill dragon. We have heard so much about it though that we are braced for trouble. With a good steel brake and a seventy-five foot picket rope fastened behind for the children to pull back on, and me boosting on the underside to help the wagon on the sidling places out of that steep windy comb, we arrived safely at the foot, though three stagecoaches had blown over in one day the week before.

We entered Lander on July 22nd, where we received our first letter and the pocketbook. The anxious one was impatiently waiting to telephone, so I was soon at that office, rejoicing to hear the dear familiar voice, even in "Hello." Then, "Are you coming home or going on?" "Going on, of course." A nervous little laugh came over the wire, then silence. A pole fell or a wire broke somewhere out on the endless plains, and our talk was over. Such hard luck. Still thankful just for the sound of my husband's voice, we hurried on.

The girls like to press curious plants in books. Apropos of books, I shudder to this day when I recall the difference between the reading planned for them and what they read. Very carefully I searched the shelves for a few choice volumes. One of Shakespeare's comedies. I would take plenty of time some rainy day to read it well, when they must like it—even the youngest; Ethics of the Dust went in, for I longed to have my dear daughter a follower of Ruskin, too. Besides it was such a little book. One of Dickens, Captain Chittenden's Yellowstone Park guide book, two or three recent Outlooks, a first year Latin in case a backward child wanted to study—of such was my collection. Well, the only book they opened was the Headless Horseman, which a chum handed the driver as we were starting. Up and down the line it went, over and over.

The responsibility and anxiety of the long trip are laying hold of me, till I'm nearly overwhelmed. Four hundred miles from home, and only one letter! What may have happened in all these weeks. Suppose a child should sicken. There's a man at home who would never forgive me should one of them be lost. Will the horses hold out? The food? Already two spokes are broken and wrapped together with baling wire. My bold driver says we shall go on if we have to drive into the park with every spoke bound up with baling wire. And the dangers anticipated did add a certain zest. "Give Ma something to fret about and she's happy," observed our twelve-year-old philosopher.

Our problems narrowed to a question of food with the Continental Divide looming in the distance. How to cook enough for all those hungry children, where bread could not be bought, and still get ahead fifteen or twenty miles a day, was a poser. The capacity of my oven was two tins of twelve biscuits each. These I filled three times at night, when darkness overtook me. That made seventy-two biscuits, three apiece every meal, but the boys wanted six and that was the problem. We caught a few fish, but saw no game from Lander on. We had gooseberry pie, all we wanted, and fresh strawberry short cake once. All grew tired of our staples—bacon, beans, corn, coffee, sardines, prunes, etc., and cold water biscuits. When the boys felt particularly cross and sarcastic they gloated aloud over the memory of Mrs. Dyer's cream biscuits. Yet it is only fair to add that keen appetites and inspiring scenery made the want of variety of food seem unimportant, even when the butter gave out.

Over the Continental Divide to Jackson Hole was a continual surprise—the road was so good, smooth, hard, well graded—thanks to Captain Chittenden. The plain just gradually lifted up from Lander Valley until it rested on the divide, two hundred miles away. The spurt that took us over the pass wasn't so gradual. But it is fine to climb a thousand feet and look about when you have mounted to 10,000 feet and gaze the crest of the continent, the Atlantic slope behind, the Pacific slope spreading before you, range after range. With intervening valley, gorge, river, lake, with the Grand Teton gleaming over all in the distance—magnificent, inspiration—your soul is filled with exaltation.

I get the grandeur of it under stress. When they called to see the clouds lift from the brow of Mount Moran I was lining up smoking hot buttermilk pancakes. Later, as the sun shot his golden lances among the fleecy mass and the woods echoed the children's hallelujahs, I was up to my elbows in the washtub, making us spick and span for the park. So, with a little, sudsy shirt in my hand, I'd run to see earth and morning meet in a burst of glory on Teton heights.

We meet so many outfits returning, from Salt Lake, Idaho, Kansas, everywhere. Few have come so far as we, though we traveled two days with families from Jewell, Kansas, who would have gone before reaching home a thousand miles farther than we. One of the men said he never had a vacation before and now he meant to have his fill. They intended to stay until the hunting season opened, to get big game.

Many of the returning outfits had great four-horse freight wagons, loaded with bedsprings, mattresses, chairs, tables, Easter bonnets, and a multitude of burdensome luxuries. "Burdensome," their careworn faces said plainly. Grateful we are to Stewart Edward White for his advice to "go light." And it is interesting to make one dish serve for six. By putting pillowcases inside of gunnysacks we carried necessary clothing without much weight or waste of space. Grocery stores are never more than three days apart so why a mess wagon? We hauled just enough canned goods over the divide to last us to Moran, that is, Allen's ranch, where all good things were to be had, even butter.

I know one young man who made the trip in company with his mother, sister, sweetheart and others, but no larger party than ours, yet he had a regular caravan, a four-horse mess wagon, phaeton, buggy, and horseman. We camped near them occasionally and saw how every night he had to be responsible for a dozen horses, see that they had good feed; and it is no picnic to watch horses in heavy timber, for they break loose and wander off. Then he had to round them all up every morning, feed oats and drive a four-horse rig all day. I must add that he kept his temper and stood the ordeal so well that his sweetheart married him soon after his return to Lander.

As we cross the borders of the wonderland each step grows more enticing, and after the many years of waiting and the long, laborious journey, I demand much.

The shady avenues of young pines, lovely Moose Falls on Snake River, climbing the divide again into the Atlantic Basin, the live beaver homes and haunts, enchanting Lewis Falls and Lake and River, the noble forests of a thousand years' growth and the pure, rich color of mountain flowers, all is satisfying. How much greater the delight of descending into Yellowstone Valley!

The wonder and charm grew until, throwing care to the winds, yet with a firm grip on the pocketbook, we yielded to a delicious abandon, sure that every anticipation would be realized. Yet it is a pokerish kind of pleasure trying to enjoy the ravings of the demons from the bottomless pit at the "Thumb."[2]

As for me I was kept busy counting the children. Every time one moved I felt certain he would stumble into a walloping loping vat of mud. That it was delicate rose, emerald or heavenly blue mud did not reassure me. The children only laughed. Even the youngest pertly informed me he had not come all the way to Yellowstone Park to fall into a mud hole. Still the horrid smells and awful groans and the gaping mouths clear to Hades aroused such emotions of terror that in sheer desperation I hurried over to the lake. Playing with silver tipped waves or silver-tipped bears were safe in comparison.

---

2 The Corthells were visiting the Paint Pots, hot springs of boiling mud, at the West Thumb of Lake Yellowstone. They entered the park by the south entrance so these would have been the first significant geothermal feature they encountered.

The children know "Wahb" and "Johnny Bear" by heart, of course, so they eagerly followed the hotel guests along the little trail to the garbage glen to find if the Thompson Seton stories are true.[3] They are all true. There was another little black Johnny Bear "who wanted to see." Another big lumbering Wahb, younger, maybe, but just as grizzly, and cinnamon bears and silver tips, growling and fighting over their food. I wasn't stampeded here as at the Thumb, for a stout fence separated us from the ferocious monsters.

Refreshed and in fine spirits we started early down the Hayden Valley, where we came in contact with the hard rules of the Park. One of them is, that always four-horse stagecoaches have the right-of-way, and you have to turn out so as to give them the safe side. That is, if you are on a steep grade you have to turn out on the precipice side, giving them the inside, no matter whether you are turning to right or left and no matter if you have eight people and they but two. We were obliged to turn out that morning for ten separate coaches. Sometimes there are twenty coaches going along fifteen minutes apart.[4]

But we didn't mind. We were too elated to mind. We had only sixteen miles to go and wanted time to enjoy every beautiful, exquisite prospect. Professor Nelson told us before starting not to fish in Yellowstone Lake or River because the fish are diseased. He said that scientists from the Smithsonian Institution had made careful study and gave it as their opinion that excretions from pelicans, which swarm on the lake, and which fish devour, contain a parasitic growth that infects the fish.

As we drove along the river's edge there were pools and shallows in which we saw hundreds of fish looking bruised and sickly, even showing naked bones, yet swimming about. Presently we passed riffles and cascades among which road workmen were fishing. They said fish that could live in a cataract were not diseased. Mr. Turnbull having only a second-hand account at best was not greatly impressed with the sick fish story, so he and our young driver were soon pulling out fine big rainbow trout. When they had a dozen we went on to lunch in a cozy meadow, dotted with lovely blue fringed

---

3 Ernest Thompson Seton was a famous naturalist, artist, and author whose books and stories about wild animals were enormously popular. He was also the founder of the Woodcraft Indians, a precursor of the Boy Scouts of America.

4 Coaches left park hotels at 15-minute intervals to allow the dust to settle on the unpaved roads. This interval was convenient for armed robbers who in 1914 held up twenty-five coaches one at a time east of Old Faithful.

gentian close by the river's edge, though just beyond we noticed a steaming and a smelling.

The small boys hardly took time to eat, for they wanted to catch big fish, too. After lunch Mr. Turnbull proceeded to examine the beautiful trout. There was a coil of worms in the flesh or entrails of every fish. Then I fled to tell the fisherman. They couldn't hear me call. I saw where their bare feet had gone around a patch of ground which appeared to be neither marsh nor sandbar—a crusty, shiny, disagreeable place. I could cut across. Not looking so much where I stepped but keeping the boys in sight, my feet burned. I knew then what it means to be over a lake of fire and brimstone. Good sprinting brought me to safety. Then we investigated the awful roaring from the cliff above.

On the side of a hill there was a great black chasm, partly filled with black mud that angrily flopped and spluttered and moaned. Around on the other side of the hill was a cavern. In it was a pool of boiling water that disappeared in the bowels of the hill, to reappear in a few moments, roaring and howling. There were other frightful mud geysers gaping like the jaws of Hades. I had walked on the crusted overflow. Again I fled fearing they would snap up my little people.

But the glory of Yellowstone Canyon speedily restored our nerves. Now are we most grandly repaid for every moment of weariness and anxiety of the journey, nearly six hundred miles long.

Tongue and pen and brush and camera are all inadequate to give a picture of the canyon, which for resplendent beauty in form and color stands unequaled, unique in the world. At Inspiration Point every soul was dumb with rapture. Even "Spring Jaws," as they call Tad, had nothing to say. He too, was enchanted, lifted to the seventh heaven, as it were, so that only twice, I think, did he squirm outside the rail over the precipice. To see him so impressed was great relief to all of us. Oh, it is wonderful to see a canyon so broad it is almost a valley, yet so deep you cannot hear a sound of the rushing torrent below; so brilliant in all the colors of the rainbow your eyes cannot bear it long; so studded with nature's architecture you see a thousand ruins of cathedrals and coliseums, and at the head of all a waterfall over three hundred feet in depth. Remember, Niagara is only one hundred sixty-five feet deep.

Of course, we remained here a day or two, sightseeing, cooking, resting, awaiting a telegram. It seemed sacrilegious to return to camp after that glorious gaze into nature's proudest wonderland and go baking beans, yet we had to have a change from Van Camp's. I wouldn't speak of it now only that is how we came to have a visit from a bear.

The beans were not done at bedtime, so I put in pine knots, thinking they would be just right for breakfast. It was so hot the stove was outside. About midnight there was a great clatter of falling stove. Sure enough, a bear had tipped it over trying to get my beans. He was trying so hard to work the combination of the oven door that he never noticed our excitement. Not until I threw things at him would he go away. On the whole, I presume, we would have been disappointed if one bear, at least, had not paid us a visit. We never thought of being afraid, but I used all my ingenuity in hiding bacon and sugar from prowling bears, every night.

Captain Chittenden built a magnificent cement bridge over cascades, just above the falls. It was receiving finishing touches as we arrived on the scene. I thought at first it was a wooden bridge, but the wood was only a frame for concrete masses of rock had been crushed in all sizes, in all dimensions. Immense floors for mixing cement were prepared and aid workmen came from every corner of the park—three hundred of them. Electric lights were strung, and for seventy consecutive hours cement and concrete poured into those wooden forms held by strong steel cables. The wood will remain all winter and next summer there will appear a splendid bridge over which tourists may cross to the far side of Yellowstone Canyon, and by that means reach the foot of the Lower Falls. Those who have, through prodigious effort, arrived at the foot say that no idea of the height is apparent to standing at the brink. Of the three hundred ten feet, one third is lost in spray.

We spent the forenoon of the next day taking a last long look into the Grand Canyon of the Yellowstone. On our way back we found at the Canyon Hotel our expected message: "Will meet you at Mammoth Hot Springs, August 8th."

Oh then we flew as fast as our faithful horses could plod, for August 8th is tomorrow and Mammoth thirty miles away.

It is love that makes the world go round after all. Beauty may exalt, but love vitalizes. The mere thought of seeing our beloved so soon lent wings to our feet and new life to our hopes and joys, so that surmounting the divide which separates Yellowstone from Norris Basin was not so much work as a needed exercise for holding down our jubilation. The prospect of losing most of my responsibilities sent my spirits floating skyward.

We camped at Apollinaris Spring in a charming grove at the edge of a grassy glen. The very air seemed resonant with human life, and presently the children discovered a large party of Wylie tourists camping in the grove beyond.[5]

They were very pleasant people, mostly schoolteachers from Fort Dodge, Iowa, and vicinity, and we spent a happy evening getting acquainted.

We arrived in Mammoth five minutes ahead of the stage from the railway station at Gardiner. How we rushed to make camp homey. The driver quickly unhitched and had the horses grazing; Daughter, Tom and Babe set the tent; Tad brought wood; Glad, water; and Mim speedily had a roaring fire; while I popped my biscuits in the oven, sliced bacon, seasoned corn, opened a jar of jam and brought on the baked beans that were left, and set the coffee simmering.

Daughter watched the fire, Glad spread the tablecloth, Mim tidied the mess box and the boys put the bedding to air in the hot sun. Then we had a moment to primp, wondering what Father would bring, for shoes and hats had seen hard service. Little Mim, sensing the hopelessness of primping said, "I wish he could bring me a new face." But he never minded our weather-beaten appearance, though we had "roughed it" for five weeks. We all looked good to him, and the wonderful "springs" reflecting the joy of the occasion gleamed in rainbow tints.

Luncheon over, the strange formations soon attracted us. Pulpit Terrace, Jupiter Terrace, Liberty Cap, Devil's Kitchen are intensely interesting—all are wonderful. These terraces are fully three hundred feet above the town, but flowing toward the town. If I lived there I should be in constant fear that a fresh new boiling spring would spout in my cellar.

We have not seen all the wonders of the park—in fact, we are just half way around, still we have reached the farthest limits and are six hundred miles from home.

---

5 William Wallace Wylie first visited Yellowstone Park in 1880 and in 1893 got permission to establish permanent camps in Yellowstone Park. He provided moderately priced tours that provided guides, transportation, and lodging in tents that were left up for the season. He promoted these tours as seeing the park "the Wylie Way."

Now a new spirit has entered camp. The businessman has come to take his family home. We have to hurry. Oats are increased three-fold and three-fold our speed. Then ho! For the geysers!

Now we must climb the hill from Mammoth, four miles long. But it is a fine smooth road of gentle, even grade and a magnificent view of snow-capped peaks, peaceful valleys and age-old forests, from Golden Gate. While the park roads are smooth as city streets, still you go up or down, up to mountain heights, down to cool, dark canyons. As a matter of course there is no road in the world like it—a road 150 miles long that passes such variety of scenery—scenery so majestic, so wonderful, so beautiful, so horrible. And several times going over divides we saw altitudes marked on mile posts over 9,000 feet.

By and by we are back in Norris Basin, taking time to look at the Devil's Frying Pan and other steaming, sputtering curiosities. At the former spot was a guide board having several notes in pencil beneath the sign addressed to his Satanic Majesty. One read, "Dear Devil: We called on you today and were right glad to find you out, whooping it up for the other sinners. Now when it comes our turn, please dear Devil, we don't want to boil in your cave or bake in your kitchen or sizzle in your frying pan give us the dynamite route—sudden and not too hot."

The Black Growler, a hideous, shrieking, hissing monster, we admire for his titanic and Satanic power, but hastily pass on to cool, solid ground after a glance at the Hurricane, a mighty steam vent whose violent gusts are like the blast of a tempest. We camped in Gibbon Meadow that night and fished in Gibbon River. The next morning we drove slowly through Gibbon Canyon in order to admire the beauty of Gibbon Falls. Then we climbed another divide so as to get down into Firehole Basin, where the "hot times" really are, as the name indicates.

We lunched on the Firehole River fully ten miles below the Lower Geyser Basin, cool mountain brooks flowing into the river between, and yet the water was unnaturally warm.

We all went wading and were greatly fooled by the extraordinary clearness of the water. I'd guess it would come knee high, and find myself in up to the waist.

As we drew up on the bank of Firehole River today, there was a steep little pitch from the road to the ground above just a deep rut. The horses could not pull evenly as one stood above it, the other below, so a whiffletree snapped clear in two.[6] That is to say, "the New Camp Spirit" took chances that the boy driver and I never did. But good luck was with us this day, too. In fifteen minutes a big freight outfit came along having an extra whiffletree that they very kindly loaned us.

I have inserted this good luck story in here because I did not want to speak of the geysers, which come next, until I could have plenty of space for a full swing at them. You would naturally think when you had seen one geyser you had seen all. But there is as much variety in their form, action, attractiveness, as in the flowers and animals of the woods beyond. Some are natural fountains having bowls of rarest beauty; some build cones above a mound of rich lace work made of many-hued flint; some shoot straight, tall columns of water; some send up showers of dew drops. Some play independently and with the regularity of clock works; some always wait for their elders to spout first.

Of the unnumbered thousands of steam vents, only the more important can be mentioned. It is nothing there to see a dozen tiny threads of steam puffing up in the middle of the road, while if we had just one in Laramie we would quickly build a summer resort around it.

The first geyser we saw in action was the Fountain, one of the finest in the Lower Basin. It is on a hill commanding a splendid view of the whole valley, and spouted a beautiful column of water ten or fifteen minutes. But its dear little neighbor, Clepsydra, which spouted immediately afterward, captured my heart. It sent up a sparkling shower of dewdrops no higher than a man's head that in the bright sunshine resembled a lovely bush loaded with gems. One cannot understand the perfect transparency of the water until he realizes that every particle of animal, vegetable, mineral solids held in solution in cold springs is here completely boiled out, steamed out and deposited long ago. To be sure there are pools so full of earthy substance that the steam only evaporates and wastes trying to purify itself—then we have the Paint Pots that have been mixing their paints a thousand years.

The most noted of these is the Mammoth Paint Pot just across the road from the Fountain Geyser. It is a pit fifty feet across, full of rich, smooth, strawberry ice cream, which somehow bubbles up six or eight feet, then drops back into exquisite roses and tulips. Quite a band of material has formed

---

6 A whiffletree distributes the force equally among the horses.

about the rim in a path soft and springy and smooth. The barefoot boys were cantering around it in great glee when I called them away, fearing one might stumble in, where he would disappear instantly, and forever. "Oh, Mamma!" said Tad, "I never had so much barefooted fun in my life!"

The Great Fountain Geyser is a mile beyond the Fountain. It is considered the chief wonder of the Lower Basin, but as I didn't see it play, we'll go on to Middle Basin, where there's something doing all the time.

Here is the famous "Hell's Half Acre," a vast seething cauldron 350 feet long and 200 feet across, 20 feet deep, with cliff-like edges on all sides but one. On that side, protected from winter's cold, and always having more than summer's heat, we found a yellow flower growing. It must have been a tropical plant, but how did it get there?

This huge boiling cauldron is now known to be a geyser and is named Excelsior. As a dynamic force it has no equal. Think of a body of water of such stupendous dimensions being hurled 200 feet in the air! Its last eruption occurred in 1888 when the volume of Firehole River was doubled. Captain Chittenden calls it a water volcano.[7]

Five hundred feet west of Excelsior is Prismatic Lake, the largest, most beautiful spring in the whole region. Over the central bowl the water is a deep blue, changing to green toward the margin; while the shallow edges are yellow, shading into orange. Outside the rim is a brilliant red deposit, fading into browns, grays, purples. It rests on a self-built mound sloping gently in all directions.

Whenever the steam lifts so that the waters are visible, the play of colors is strikingly vivid. We were here when the sun was low so possibly the brilliant coloring was more dazzling than in midday.

Turquoise Spring nearby is a quiescent pool 100 feet across, remarkable for its lovely transparent blue. When Excelsior played, the water in Turquoise sank ten feet and didn't recover its volume for a year. We made camp here just as quick as we could find a cool, safe spot, for we wanted the beauty of Prismatic Lake to sink deep, but unconsciously, the horror of "Hell's Half Acre" pressed deeper.

---

7 The Excelsior was the largest geyser in the world that threw a 300-foot curtain of water as high as 300 feet several times in the late nineteenth century. Long dormant, it reactivated briefly in the summer of 1985, throwing water 60 feet high.

Up before sun the next morning such a weird, ghostly spectacle met us. Apparently, smoke stacks and steam engines are sending their cloudy columns above the dark foliage in all directions—yet no cities, no factories, only the silence of the forest.

A big day lies before us, we know we are approaching the climax of the park's wonders. Old Faithful, "The Guardian of the Valley," will appear around the next bend.

As we turn the corner and the Upper Basin spreads before us we instinctively exclaim, "Dante's Inferno!" Here grouped, within a mile's space are the grandest, mightiest geysers in the world, and silent pools of scalding water, unequaled in beauty of form and delicacy of coloring. The entire valley is covered with a gray-white sepulchral deposit that is ghastly; clouds of vapor hang shroud-like above it; the earth trembles with a strange rumbling, the air is heavy with sulphur fumes and all vegetable life is extinct; though the forest presses like a dark fringe close around and emphasizes the ghastly look of death and destruction. To be sure the other basins were similar, but this is greater in degree, a culmination of it all, probably older than all.

The next thing to take the tourist's eye was the very appropriate nomenclature: Jewel Geyser, Biscuit Basin, Sapphire Pool, the Morning Glory, the Sponge, the Sawmill, Grotto, Castle, Giant, Punchbowl. Beyond all at the head of the valley on the summit of a self-made mound on a hill, stands Old Faithful. Captain Chittenden says, "Any other geyser, any five other geysers could be erased from the list better than part with Old Faithful." The Giant, Giantess, Grand, Splendid, Excelsior have more powerful eruptions. The Bee Hive is more artistic. Great Fountain has a more wonderful formation. But Old Faithful partakes in a high degree of all of these characteristics, and in addition has the invaluable quality of periodicity of action. It is in fact the most perfect of all known geysers. To it fell the honor of welcoming civilized man to this region. It was the first geyser named. In its eruption this geyser is very fascinating. Its graceful column rises with ease, to a height of 150 feet. The steam when carried laterally by a gentle breeze unfurls itself like an enormous flag from its watery standard.

With an average interval of sixty-five minutes it varies little either way. Night and day, winter and summer, seen and unseen, this tremendous fountain has been playing for untold ages.[8]

---

8 The interval between Old Faithful eruptions has lengthened over time. It is now about 95 minutes.

Only in thousands of years can its lifetime be reckoned; for the visible work it has wrought at its present infinitely slow rate of progress, fairly appalls the inquirer who seeks to learn its real age.

Its daily work is enormous. The United States Geological Survey reports show the outpour for an average eruption to be not less than 1,500,000 gallons, which gives 33,225,300 gallons per day.

"The combination of conditions by which the supply of heat and water and the form of the tube are so perfectly adapted to their work, that even a chronometer is scarcely more regular in its action, is one of the miracles of nature."

We camped across the road from Old Faithful and saw it play five times; but we shouldn't have stopped there, we were taking chances. The park rules are very strict in regard to trespass on the formations, and thereby hangs a tale: But then, you would not expect such a large family to pass among a whole valley full of yawning gulfs and smiling springs and shooting geysers, absorbed until they forgot time and place and circumstance and not have something happen, would you? Since none of them fell into a hot spring what could matter?

Well, "The New Camp Spirit" got arrested! And that mattered a good deal.

The horses found feed scarce in the very heavy timber so came into the open where the road lay. Just across, on forbidden territory, was a bunch of grass that poor Star wanted. Now he didn't intend to swallow Old Faithful, or tramp on its flinty surroundings. We were busy spreading a good, hot dinner on the tablecloth, so failed to notice Star quite quick enough. Presently we saw, and sent a boy to drive him back, but a soldier on horseback got ahead of him, and swearing like a trooper at boy and horse, he came thundering up saying, "Consider yourself under arrest, sir, and come with me!" In his very very sweetest manner and most persuasive tone, Mr. Corthell asked, "May I finish my dinner first?" "Well, yes sir," somewhat mollified. And he sullenly stood in the background.

But dinner had lost its savor. This is an experience we had nowhere reckoned on. What if it meant jail—forgotten pocketbooks, broken wagons, floods, nothing ever created such consternation as this. But we didn't fall into a panic. The chief victim was so placid, so serene, even sweetly content, that the example set composed the rest of us. Before the walk to headquarters was over, sweetness won the day, so the fine was only two dollars when it might have been a hundred. From this point on the "New Camp Spirit" took no more chances and always put out his fires.

Again we cross the continental divide and are on the Pacific slope eight or ten miles, whence we have a magnificent view of Shoshone Lake and Teton Mountains. It is said there is another geyser system on Shoshone Lake, second only to that on Firehole River, but this is one of the side trips made on horseback which we cannot take. So ascending the divide again we drop down the Atlantic slope toward Yellowstone Valley. This time the Paint Pots at the Thumb really are beautiful and fascinating. Here is where you pull a fish out of the lake and throw it into a boiling spring, without moving.[9]

As we are going home over the new Cody road which begins at the wooden bridge over the Yellowstone River at its head, or where the lake pours into the river, why of course, we must detour to the canyon. I have quite a curiosity to know if Mud Volcano, Devil's Cave, etc., will appear so formidable to me as before. My husband thinks they are frightful—the most horrible sights he has met. I believe I put Hell's Half Acre first, in the list of my horrible, Black Growler second; and Mud Volcano third.

Like everybody else, we loved Old Faithful and the Morning Glory, we feared Excelsior, we admired the Giant, Bee Hive, Punch Bowl and a hundred other yawning chasms and smiling springs and spouting geysers. But the horrible rumbling as if an earthquake were imminent and the smell of brimstone made me eager to get my brood into the valley of safety beyond the Yellowstone.

We left the park for Laramie over a new road recently completed by Captain Chittenden, through Sylvan Pass and Shoshone Canyon to Cody. This is the crowning joy of the trip. The park swarmed with people. Wherever we pitched our tent, there hundreds had camped before us, to say nothing of the crowded hotels and Wylie tourists. But here in the heart of the mountain forest surely we are the first white woman and children to go over the trail, to fish in Sylvan Lake, to climb Grizzly Peak, to camp within the sacred haunts of Wahb, once lord of the Wind River Range.

Altogether we traveled twelve hundred miles, stood the journey well and never, never had such a wonderful delightful summer. One must love the life

---

9 Cooking fish in hot springs without removing them from the line is possible in several places in the park. The most famous is the Fishing Cone on the edge of Lake Yellowstone.

to say that, must crave the outdoors and thrive on it. The sand was never too deep, the waters too high or the way too long. Every obstruction made the goal a dearer prize and we have lived our precious summer over and over.

Cold, thirst, hunger, fatigue, loneliness, I wanted the children to feel them all deeply, that their sympathy with the deprivation and isolation of the noble hearted army who blaze the way for civilization may be keen, true and sometimes helpful.

It is a trip anybody can take. It cost us only $25 apiece for the two months outing. We met people from Kansas and Salt Lake traveling just as we were. We had $15 worth of medicine along and never took a dose. The ammonia bottle was broken, also the camphor. The children emptied the witch hazel out in order to put specimens in. They plastered the arnica salve on the horses, and the dog ate the cold cream, and we shared our eight bottles of mosquito dope with ranchmen where we stopped. The wagon created some amusement on our arrival, for it bore the inscription, "July 4th, Park or Bust" on one side, and "September first, Park and Busted!" on the other. The children know their State as no book could teach them, and will have lifelong memories of the grandest scenes the world can produce.

Seeing Yellowstone "The Wylie Way"

Hester Henshall—1903

Hester Ferguson Henshall was an amateur botanist and botanical artist. She co-authored a book, Common Names of Montana Plants, *and more than one thousand of her paintings of wildflowers are collected in twelve bound volumes at the Lloyd Library and Museum in Cincinnati.*

Hester was married to Dr. James Henshall, who was director of the federal fish hatchery in the mouth of Bridger Canyon just north of Bozeman. Dr. Henshall was a physician, but he made his name as an angler and fish biologist, and his Book of the Black Bass, *published in 1881, is still in print.*

The Henshalls left the comfortable cottage at the fish hatchery and travelled to the park by train. By 1903 railroad tracks had reached the edge of Yellowstone Park at Gardiner, Montana.

They toured Yellowstone "The Wylie Way." That is, with Wylie Permanent Camping Company, which offered tourists a comprehensive package that included transportation, food, and lodging in tents that were put up in the Spring and left up for the season. The tour included a steamboat cruise across Yellowstone Lake.

Hester Ferguson Henshall's diary, Trip Through the Yellowstone National Park, Bozeman, Montana, August 10, 1903, *is illustrated with photographs, clippings, and Henshall's watercolors and drawings. It is in the collection of the Montana Historical Society.*

* * * *

Monday, August 10. We were to rise at 4:30 am to get ready for the train at Bozeman, en route to Gardiner, Montana, on the way to the Yellowstone National Park, but overslept, so all was hurry and bustle to get ready for town and the train. I drank a cup of coffee and Mary put some fried chicken and biscuits into the lunch basket for me. The drive to town in the early morning was lovely. We made the train all right, which fortunately was on time. We met a number of people also going to the park. We arrived at Livingston, Montana, in an hour and greatly admired the beautiful new station, one of the handsomest in the union.[1] Here we changed cars for Gardiner, boarding the "Park Train." Livingston is a clean-looking town, seems as if freshly washed and painted, though the wind sweeping down the Yellowstone River canyon is something terrible, blowing half a gale nearly every day. There are several curio stores in the town, so Doctor told me to walk over and see the lovely things for sale. Finally, we took the train for Gardiner, the terminus of the branch road, five miles from the park. It was a well-filled train too. If all these people are going to the park—Gracious!!! The scenery along the route, up the Yellowstone River, is very interesting and the wild flowers are in such quantities—sunflowers, golden rod, cleome, lupines, and sand lilies, both yellow and white. How I wish I could pick them! (Before we reached Livingston we saw the immense flume at Bear Canyon through which the railroad ties, lumber and shingles are carried from the mountains to the railroad.)

At Horr, on the Yellowstone, we saw the long line of coke ovens that prepare coke for the great smelting works at Butte and Anaconda. Next we saw the "Devil's Slide" near Cinnabar. It is of red earth, down a precipitous mountain ride, running between two walls of trap rock about one hundred yards apart, the slide being probably a half mile in extent—too steep for a comfortable toboggan slide. The name Cinnabar was no doubt suggested by the beautiful red rocks in the vicinity of the town.[2] We reached Gardiner, the end of our journey, in a short time. Here the Yellowstone Park coaches pick us up. They have four or six horses and are quite dashing in appearance. We took a "Wylie" coach and were driven to the "Wylie House." The matron in charge, Mrs. Taylor of Bozeman, met us. We took lunch there. Most of the tourists left their trunks and superfluous baggage to be stored until their return and put on clothing suitable for park travel. At one o'clock we took the coach for Mammoth Hot Springs, five miles distant, passing under the great stone arch, which was recently erected. The wall on each side is being built. It is a very plain, massive piece of masonry, the entrance to the park. A tablet at the

---

1 Passenger train service from Livingston, Montana, to Yellowstone Park began in 1883. The train station Mrs. Henshall referred to was built in 1902. It is now a museum.

2 The reddish colors in this area are caused by rust (iron oxide) rather than cinnabar (mercury sulfide).

The Handkerchief Pool, where people could drop in small items and have them cleaned, used to be one of Yellowstone Park's favorite features. It is no longer active because of years of abuse by tourists.
NATIONAL PARK SERVICE.

top is inscribed: "For the Benefit and Enjoyment of the People." The corner stone was laid last spring by President Roosevelt.

In our coach were Mrs. Livingston of Nebraska, Mrs. Littfield of Bozeman, Montana, Miss Brush of Wisconsin, Dr. Donaldson of Iowa, Mr. And Mrs. Albee of Minnesota, the Doctor and I, with our baggage in the boot.

Before starting there was a violent storm of hail, rain, and wind, which abated somewhat but while on our way we had frequent showers. The storm curtains on the windward side were lowered so we could still observe the wonders on the lee side. At Gardiner the road leaves the Yellowstone River and follows the Gardiner River through the canyon for about two miles. This river is the wildest, maddest stream I ever saw, full of immense rocks and great boulders among which the stream goes rushing, boiling, and foaming along, making a great noise and uproar. It is a wild and fierce river but so clear. To one accustomed to the discolored streams of the Mississippi valley, its crystal clearness is a marvel. All along the roads through the park are mileposts giving the distances each way and the altitude. In Gardiner Canyon we saw Eagles' Nest rock. We saw the nest on a high pinnacle but not the eaglets. Some of the cliffs near this rock are fully 1,500 feet above the roadway—more than a quarter mile straight up. Across Gardiner River Mount Everts, a long, high ridge, loomed up. In the distance glimpses were caught of Bunsen's Peak and Electric Peak.

Upon arriving at the Mammoth Hot Springs Hotel we went on to the curio store where we saw all sorts of characteristic articles, as horseshoes, pine cones, cups, vases, etc., all coated with incrustations of lime from placing them in the water of the springs. They are white as snow and quite pretty. One man was filling bottles with sand of different colors and in various patterns and even forming pictures of trees, bears, deer, etc. The sand is found in the park, mostly from the Grand Canyon and varies from black obsidian sand to such colors as dark and light red, ochre, and Naples yellow to white.

While we were at this store there occurred a heavy storm of hail and rain. As I was more interested in the wonderful scenery than in curios, I spent most of the interval of waiting on the little rustic porch. During the height of the storm, I observed a number of tourists on the top of the Terrace calmly viewing its beauties. There is a military post here, Fort Yellowstone, the garrison of the park. The officers' quarters are quite neat and pretty dwellings. I was fascinated by the great terraced hill built up by the Mammoth Hot Springs and listening to the rush of many waters. This eminence is about 300 feet high, formed in regular terraces, one above the other, with hot water flowing over. At the base, on level ground, is a dome or pillar called the "Liberty Cap," over 50 feet high and about 20 feet in diameter. The formation of the terraces is calcareous, and is said to be built up at the rate of one-sixteenth an inch in four days.

When the rain was over we entered our coach and were driven to the top of the terraces where we alighted to view the wonders. I scarcely know how to describe the "formation", it looks so delicate and fragile and yet it bears one's weight like solid rock. The hot water overflows the pools and reservoirs gently forming facings and borders of marvelous patterns, as if carved, some white as snow, some yellows, orange, red, or brown. There are a number of pools of various sizes and shapes, all smoking and steaming. Across the road is Lookout Hill, surmounted by a blockhouse and utilized as a weather signal station.

Journeying on we soon came to the "Hoodoos," on each of the steep ascents of the road. This region is well-named, being the strangest and oddest collection of rocks imaginable, as if all the rocks left over after the cliffs and mountains were finished were dumped without plan or method into these gorges. They are of all shapes and sizes and stand in all manner of attitudes, singly and in groups: queer, weird, grotesque, and fantastic. The wind moans through the narrow passages like the voices of lost spirits.

Still ascending we came to the Golden Gate and the viaduct around the great cliff. On one side of the roadway, close to the coach, rises a vertical yellow rock to the height of two or three hundred feet and on the other side, down, down, down is the river. We got out of the coach for a better view. A low parapet protects the roadway and by looking back over it one can see the great stone arches that support the viaduct. At the head of the gorge is a beautiful little cascade, the Rustic Falls. After reaching the top of the grade we soon came to Swan Lake on which numerous waterfowl floated. Doctor said they were swans but I could not distinguish them.

At last we came to Willow Park station, our camp for the night. Just imagine a group of tents arranged so as to form a small village. Each tent had a wooden floor, a stove, a wood box full of wood, a bench with a row of candles, and water pitchers. Our tent was Number 6 and was divided into four rooms by screens or cloth partitions. In each room was a curtained box for a washstand, a small mirror somewhat wavy on the surface, some towels, and soap. Nails were driven in the top of the partition frame on which to hang our clothes. There were four camp chairs in the hall of the tent. Occupying our tent were Mrs. Littlefield, Mrs. Livingston, Miss Brush, the Doctor and I. Here we proceeded to rid ourselves of dust, to wash and comb, and get ready for dinner. Everyone was hungry and when the bell, or triangle sounded we wended our way to a large tent in which were two long tables all filled with good food, well cooked and served. After dinner we came out to find a jolly, large, campfire in the space between the tents. On a bench beneath a large tree was a bench with two pails of water and above them was a sign with the legend "Water; Plain and Polly." The plain water comes from the cold stream nearby and the "Polly" from an Apollinaris Spring just across the road. The latter tastes much like the real article and makes a capital lemonade. Around the cheerful fire we soon became acquainted with the others of our party. The matron, Miss Doyle, gave several recitations in good style. There was a small cabinet organ produced from the dining tent. When the Doctor was called on for his share of the entertainment, he sang several songs. We were very tired and soon began to think of retiring when someone suggested that we have a look at the bears. Accordingly, we proceeded to the place of deposit of kitchen refuse, the dump, where we saw an old black bear with two cubs and soon another one appeared.[3] Our curiosity in this direction being fully satisfied we sought our comfortable tent where we were soon in the land of dreams, but not a more wonderful one that the famous "Park."

Tuesday, August 11, 1903: I was awakened by the entrance of a boy with hot water, who also made a fire in the stove for the morning was quite cold, with frost. The Doctor arose and shaved while I sat up in bed and dressed my hair. I had such a good night's rest. The bed was so comfortable, with what I call Cuban blankets, mixed cotton and wool, for sheets and more than enough of comfortables. As soon as we were dressed the huge triangle rang for breakfast. On emerging from our tent we were welcomed by a blazing campfire in the square which we enjoyed for a few minutes but our appetites were too sharp to linger long and we repaired to the dining tent which we found very comfortable, being heated by a large stove. There had been a fierce hailstorm during the night accompanied by thunder but we were warm and snug in bed and did not realize it. When the Doctor spoke of it at breakfast it appeared that scarcely anyone had heard the commotion. Talk of the "seven sleepers!" There were stories of the boys being up in the night driving off the marauding bears that tried to break into the stores of the supply tent. Everyone seemed so bright and joyous this morning and all had their appetites with judging from the onslaught on the well-cooked viands. Who could blame the bears! As we had a little spare time before the coach starting, I went in search of wild flowers hoping to secure a "white" aconite (monkshood) and some Shandon bells. While peering about I heard a crashing in the underbrush and, looking up, I beheld a great bear coming toward me!! Having no further interest in flowers, I fairly flew back to camp. Doctor assured me that the bear would not have harmed me but I did not care to prove it. I had gathered

---

3 Watching bears at the dump became an essential part of any trip to Yellowstone Park when hotels began dumping garbage nearby in the 1880s. The practice remained until the 1960s when garbage was locked up.

The Steamboat Zilla took tourists like Hester Henshall across Lake Yellowstone with a stop at Dot Island where they could see wild animals in a zoo.
NATIONAL PARK SERVICE.

some monkshood, harebells, fireweed, bells of Shandon, Mertensia and some
others.

At eight o'clock the coaches were ready. In the coach were eleven tourists
and the driver. In our surrey were Mrs. Littlefield, Doctor, and I. Others clamored for a place in the surrey—Miss Brush, Mrs. Albee, and Mrs. Livingston.
They said they wanted to ride with someone who knew something, meaning
the Doctor of course. I was compelled to settle the matter and decided to
take Mrs. Littlefield with us as she was such a little woman and quite old.
On this trip we had a very good driver, Mr. Griffith, a Bozeman College boy,
who is taking a three-year course in civil engineering. We found him very
gentlemanly and obliging. He proved that there is a great difference between
a young man who is striving for an education and makes what he can during
his vacation and a young man who does not work in a perfunctory manner
for what pay and tips there is in it. He was much interested in my talk on wild
flowers and the Doctor's remarks on natural history. Soon after we started the

road wound around Obsidian Cliff. This is a sheer mountain of what I would call black glass, which is black, shining, and opaque with occasional streaks of other colors. When the sun shines on this cliff it glistens like a hundred mirrors. When making the road around it great fires were kindled against it until very hot, then water was dashed on it causing it to break into fragments. No other plan was feasible for breaking it. The road thus constructed is almost like one of glass and said to be the only one in the world. One might wonder where the fuel for these great fires was obtained but the question is easily answered in the masses of fallen timber along the road, pine and spruce that does not rot for ages. We are told that the Indians in time past obtained the material for their arrowheads from Obsidian Cliff. (When we were camping at Soda Butte Lake in the northeast corner of the park some years ago, while searching for wild flowers I found a beautiful and perfect arrow head of obsidian and feel more proud than ever of my "treasure trove.")

Beaver Lake is on the opposite side of the roadway from the cliff. The houses and dams of the beavers are still there and though we saw many wild geese and ducks we did not get sight of a beaver. Farther along we came to the beautiful Twin Lakes and then the Roaring Mountain, so called owing to the great jets of steam issuing from the surface, accompanied by a roaring as of several railroad trains rattling over trestle bridges. Then we came in sight of the Devil's Frying Pan, the steam hissing out of numberless fissures in the bottom of a shallow depression of about an acre in extent. It is a gruesome spectacle. We are now in the Norris Geyser Basin. There are so many wonderful things to see that I am afraid I will get terribly mixed in telling them. If there were but one geyser to see and study in all its aspects and to describe it would be comparatively easy, but so many, alack!

The first real geyser we encounter is the Constant, so called because it spouts nearly every minute, throwing jets of water and steam to a height of forty feet with most of the water running back into the pool or crater. Next was the Hurricane and well named for the steam rushes out of a rent in the ground with the sound of a roaring and violent storm. But the Black Growler is one of the most terrifying and fearsome things in the park. It caused a cold streak to run down my back and caused a wild sensation in my head. It throws out little water but torrents of steam rush out from a cave-like aperture with such a thunderous roar that it almost deafens one. It is continuous and one cannot help wishing it would cease if but for a moment. Here we also saw the Emerald Pool, the walls of which are like sulphur-colored coral. There are a number of small geysers, whose names I cannot recall and whose interest seems to be lost in comparison of those much larger, yet they are none-the-less wonderful studied alone. From the Norris Geyser Basin we took up our journey along the Gibbon River to the Fountain Hotel. The river flows through a wild and picturesque canyon with high, rocky crags, and cliffs, some crowned with forest of pine and fir with numerous wild flowers. Here I gathered the red monkey flower and the Grass of Parnassus. On our side of the canyon flowed the river, a wild, rushing, merry stream winding and twisting among the huge rocks in its bed and pitching down the declivities covered with froth and foam. By and by we suddenly came upon our lunch station which I was glad to see. The ladies of our party were shown to a tent where we could rid ourselves of the dust and make a partial toilet. Then we had luncheon. I remember we had such a good soup and that the table was adorned with such beautiful bunches of flowers—fireweed, aconite, gentian, wild geranium, and many others. I have not spoken of the gentian, which grows in such profusion along the Gibbon meadows, marvels of beauty. I did not gather all that I wished because I could not take care of them and think it wrong to waste wild flowers. One should not gather more than can be utilized; rather let them grow. I also saw the graceful yellow columbine growing beside the rocks. After luncheon some of us wandered off after the floral beauties and some to take photos. Everyone had become interested in gathering wild flowers, even Dr. Donaldson. The spirit of collecting had broken out as suddenly as do new geysers and paint pots in the park. I found a new wild garlic or rather one new to my collection. The others would bring me their collections to name, which I was not always able to do though I could give the family and genus. We were startled by Miss Lillian Ehlert rushing into the camp crying, "Look at me! I'm soaking wet! I got into quicksand up to my waist! The kids had to pull me out." Her grip had to be taken from the boot of the coach so that she could change her clothes. The matron of the camp hung her wet skirt, etc. behind the range to dry.

Miss Ehlert was very venturesome; always getting into trouble. Doctor named her the "awful girl" (orphan girl) and suggested that a guardian be appointed for her. Her sister said, "Well, doctor, I know no one so competent as you and I will be only too glad to resign in your favor." But he said, "I have one orphan already to take care of," meaning me.

145

As soon as Miss Ehlert's clothes were dry we resumed our journey. We shortly came to the Gibbon Falls, a very beautiful one as viewed from the road and about 80 feet high. We drank water from the Iron Spring on the bank of the river and endeavored in other ways to overcome the drowsiness, which seemed to affect even our drive. The road over the high plateau between Gibbon and Firehole Rivers is known as "Sleepy Hollow." The monotonous drive in the noonday is sure to make one sleepy.

At last we came to Firehole River, so-called because of the many geysers along its banks throwing out steam and water. Toward evening we saw the Morning Glory pool, which Doctor thinks the most beautiful one in the parks. We arrived at last at the Fountain Hotel. Near at hand is the Fountain Geyser, which is considered one of the most remarkable owing to its peculiar formation. Its cone is quite high, surrounding a large irregular pool of boiling water, which at certain intervals is thrown high in the air. After viewing the beautiful Beryl Spring we came to the wonder of wonders for me, the Paint Pots. These are craters or openings filled with soft, smooth mud, like fine white mortar. How long have they been there? Ages and ages; boiling, bubbling, puffing, and making beautiful rings and lilies in the pink and white mud. I saw one into which a lady had fallen a few years ago. Her daughter, in trying to rescue her, slipped in also and they both were terribly scalded. They were taken to the sanitarium in Bozeman where the mother died. I soon missed Doctor and was very much frightened but he returned in a few minutes with a handful of "geyser eggs," one for each lady in our party. He would not tell where he found them as it is forbidden to take specimens from the park. In the Midway Basin we came to Excelsior Geyser, once the grandest in the parks but it blew out its crater and has not spouted for several years.[4] It is not a great abyss filled with boiling water, deep blue in color but one can hardly get a glimpse of it owing to the dense steam. Near it are Prismatic Lake and Turquoise Pool, though we only saw shades of blue and green.

Resuming our journey up the Firehole River we came at eventide to the Morning Glory Pool, previously mentioned. Its outline and beautiful colors bring to mind a morning glory of exquisite hues. Next, we came to the Fan Geyser, the Mortar, and Riverside Geysers. Though none were in action, all

---

4 The Excelsior was the largest geyser in the world that threw a 300-foot curtain of water as high as 300 feet several times in the late nineteenth century. Long dormant, it reactivated briefly in the summer of 1985 throwing water 60 feet high.

were steaming and hissing. We drove across the bridge over Firehole River just below the Riverside and soon arrived at our camp for the night called Geyser Camp. The tents at this camp are named for the different geysers and other wonders of the park. Dr. Donaldson and the "kids," Marshall Levy and Charles Dugan occupied "The Growler." The dining room was styled "The Biscuit Basin." Our tent was "The Daisy." We could see the Daisy Geyser from the door of our tent. It played at frequent intervals and was always roaring and hissing. Near at hand was the dome of an extinct geyser some twelve feet high and white as snow with a constant thread of steam issuing from its peak. We were promised a sight of the Giant Geyser playing, one of the grandest sights of the park.

We were ready and Oh, so anxious, for dinner. There was another party who came in the day before and having seen the sights was to leave the next morning. One of the pleasant features of the park trip is meeting so many tourists. There are several other outfits beside the Wylie and the Transportation Company though they do not maintain permanent camps like Wylie but camp wherever there is a suitable place and usually break camp every day. Then there are the independent tourists who travel in their own conveyances and have their own camping outfit or stop at Wylie's permanent camps or at the hotels of the Transportation Company. The independent campers are called "sagebrush tourists" in ridicule. But, let me say that I would like to go as a sagebrush tourist to do as I pleased, to go or stop whenever the spirit moved me, to fish, and sketch, and loiter, and meander like the lotus-eaters. For though I took my colors and sketching material with me, I was too tired when we reached camp to even lift my hands let alone trying to sketch. As a sagebrush tourist I would have had strength and time for everything.

Soon we were called to dinner but there were many wonderful things to see that we were loath to go though hungry as bears. We are now in the Upper Geyser Basin. Have I said that it freezes a little almost every night in the park? Well, it does. As soon as the sun goes down it is cold. Then the great camp fire is kindled in the square before the tents and soon all are gathered around its cheerful blaze; no not all for some of the party whom even the jolly camp fire could not entice wandered off, some to the Riverside Geyser, some to watch the Giant, and others to visit the Daisy for there is a long twilight. I was too tired to do anything but luxuriate in the brightness and warmth of the campfire. There was a palmist with the "other" party who read one's fate for ten cents each. Even the occult and mysterious could not tempt me from my camp chair. Doctor sang several songs to the accompaniment of a wheezy cabinet organ and a man played several characteristic pieces on the violin and played them well though he was a teamster. Soon after I went to our tent and found that Mrs. Littlefield had started a fire in the stove and was taking a bath in her compartment. I made preparations to retire and sat up in bed to comb my hair. I do not know when I fell asleep but sometime during the process for in the morning when I awoke my hair was unkempt, hairpins, comb, and brush under my back and everywhere. We had hot geyser water to wash in and a good fire was in the stove. We did not have to hurry out for breakfast as we were to remain here all day. I heard the other party of tourists depart.

Wednesday, August 12th: A good night's rest, a good breakfast, and a lovely morning. In a half hour from the rising gong the triangle rang its merry rattle for breakfast. At 8 o'clock we were in the surrey and the rest of our party was in the coach on our way to view the wonders of the Upper Geyser Basin, personally conducted by the superintendent of the camp. We saw the Riverside Geyser play, saw the rainbow in its spray for the sun was just right, showing the bridge over the river through the iridescent arch. A pair of horses was drinking at the brink near the bridge. Oh, the wonder and beauty of it all. Just at first, when the water and steam burst out, cracking and sputtering, it reminded me, unaccountably, of a fire engine playing as it jetted and jerked forth steam and water with great force. I was so satisfied with the grand view that I would have been content to have seen no more. Our Kodak friends said they obtained very fine views. Next we saw the Giant, the Turban, and the Grand. The Lioness and Cubs did not play, but their craters with the water seething and boiling were wonderful for mortal eyes. We next came to the Sawmill. This geyser makes a terrific, hissing sound, much like a huge buzz saw ripping through a great saw log. Next came the Butterfly Pool with outspread wings decorated with many colors: yellows, browns, and reds, making the illusion almost perfect. We next were taken to the Ear, a pool shaped wonderfully like a human ear.

Next in order was the Giantess Geyser, which, however, was not in a playful mood. Then the Beehive Geyser, which has a cone shape like the old-fashioned English straw beehive except that the hole is at the top instead of the bottom and hot steam issues from it and not the little busy bee. It

148

is the most perfect shape from an artistic viewpoint of any geyser in the park. Next we came to the military post where President Roosevelt quartered while touring the park last spring on snowshoes. We were permitted to look through the closed window of one of the shacks at the cot he occupied at night. Among us were some who viewed it as a religious devotee at a holy shrine and almost hold their breath as they gazed at the cot with its red blanket. It seemed to interest them more than the wonders of the park; but the Doctor was not one of them, I assure you. The one votive offering that pleased me most was a great bucket of ice-cold water on a bench outside the shack. It tasted much like the delicious spring water at home. There is a novel water carrier at this Post whereby a cask, hung on a wire rope, hauls up the water from the Firehole River. I should think some such laborsaving device would be needed if all the tourists were as thirsty as we were. The hero worshippers said it made them more thirsty to know that they were drinking the same water and perhaps from the same cup as served President Roosevelt.

Here we crossed the bridge over the river and proceeded to old Faithful Geyser. So much has been written about "Old Faithful" that I hardly know what to say. I know we waited, as did many others, in the hot sunshine a long time for it to play. It is true there were benches to sit on and rest, for which I was truly thankful, but "Tell is not in the streets of Askelton." I had been quite willing to leave it unseen for I was a-weary, a-weary with our long tramp of the morning. Now I am glad I did not say anything about my being so tired. I could not go until the others went so concluded not to make myself a nuisance by worrying Doctor and the rest of the party. When Old Faithful burst forth in all his glory, higher and higher and still higher in the air that feeling vanished. The great volume of water with all its whiteness showing golden and all prismatic tints of the rainbow, seemed indeed a living fountain of iridescence. "The wind bloweth where it listeth; thou hearest the sound thereof but canst not tell whence it cometh nor whither it goeth."[5] The geyser is something like the wind; it rises, it spouts, and is gone, only to begin all over again when it listeth. Old Faithful differs from most of the geysers in that it listeth to be quite regular in its performance. Never has it disappointed waiting crowds of admirers. Every sixty-three minutes he burst forth in his beautiful fury. The crater is on the summit of a hill-shaped cone some twelve

---

5 Verse from the King James Bible, John 3:8.

feet above the level of the ground and sloped off gradually with pools of clear, crystal water flowing down the sides.

The guidebook says, "A column of hot water is thrown 150 feet in the air." Leaving Old Faithful we drove to the curio store near at hand. I think most of our party forgot geysers, pools, cascades and everything else when looking at the exquisite things one could buy. I looked at them all, admired and was interested, but again went outside to gaze at things one could not buy for money. I noticed the rustic porch and veranda of the store, so simply, quaintly, and beautifully made of young fir trees. The branches were lopped off some four or six inches from the trunk and the whole denuded of the bark. All of the posts and grill were made in this manner and I do not know when any veranda pleased more; so very appropriate for a home in the country. Some of our party bought themselves rich in treasures; Navajo blankets, belts, fobs, tobacco bags of beadwork; moccasins, spoons, cups, bows and arrows, flints, and oh so many things. As I had most of such articles and had no space to carry them, I did not purchase anything.

We then drove back to camp, viewing on the way the Castle Geyser where we were taken in a group by our Kodak people. The castle did not spout but the high walls of its crater and the tinted pools of boiling water repaid us for climbing around and up to its summit. The next object of interest was the Punch Bowl, which is not a geyser but a beautiful pool of boiling water. The basin is some five feet high and the water seethes and boils and falls over its brim. I think it is one of the prettiest and the most interesting in the park. Then came the lovely Sunset Lake with its varied tints and after that the Handkerchief Pool reminding one of a great pot of boiling water, seething, roaring, and bubbling, then issuing clouds of steam with a washday odor. Miss Lillian Ehlert, of course, must put her handkerchief in the pool.[6] We gathered around to watch it. It floated awhile, circling the pool, and then suddenly disappeared out of sight down a sucking eddy. We watched and waited, thinking it has gone forever, but it hadn't and popped up in another part of the pool and floated once more on the surface. It was then taken out with a stick to be gazed upon by all of the party with something akin to awe. We wondered where it had been when lost to sight and what it had seen and

---

6 The Handkerchief Pool was one of the most popular attractions in the park in the decades around 1900. The spring was damaged by tourists throwing large items in it and is now dormant.

undergone. What a tale it could tell if gifted with speech. Miss Ehlert simply said, "No checky, no washee, but I got it all the same."

Our next stopping place was at the Black Sand Basin, an immense pool with sloping sides composed of black obsidian sand, but the other slope is rather of sand(??) of roses tint. In one place the water has cut through the bank and discharges the hot water which has formed a coating of marvelous coloring from creamy white to pink, terra cotta, olive-green and a neutral tint with reddish streaks.

We then drove back to camp and made ready for luncheon for all were tired though full of talk and very hungry. After luncheon some of the party walked a mile through the woods to Biscuit Basin. Mrs. Livingston and I were too tired to make the effort and pressed the flowers we had gathered. After we had rested we walked a short distance to an extinct geyser called the White Pyramid, which we had viewed daily from our tent. When the others returned and saw my flower press with its specimens, they begged the cook for some empty cracker boxes to make presses for those they had gathered.

The White Pyramid just mentioned is a snow-white cone, some 12 or 15 feet high with a faint wreath of smoke rising from the top. We clambered to the summit to view the crater. The sides of the cone were quite steep and covered with a lime-like substance which made the ascent difficult as it slid from under our feet and was also pretty warm so that we felt the heat through our shoes. Nothing of special interest was to be seen but our curiosity was satisfied. We then wandered through the pine woods in search of wild flowers. I had the good fortune to find the "gray rosette" in bloom, a plant I had found two years before when en route to Henry's Lake in Idaho. It was a delightful surprise to me. There were great quantities of it; some not yet in bloom. However, on the slender stalks of others some six inches tall, springing from the gray rosette were the blossoms resembling pink daisies. Having now the flowers and rootstalk I was enabled to find its name which is Chenmactes Douglassii alpine. Glad? Well, yes. I found another little plant that closely resembled Douglassii Montana; these two were all that were new to me. There were masses of "umbrella plants: green, yellow, and white." The spot was a veritable flower garden. By the time we reached camp it was dinnertime. After dining, we sat around the cheerful campfire, some talking, some writing, others writing letters and postal cards by the light of the bright fire. Most of us turned in early. We were to leave camp at 7:00 a.m. the next morning.

Thursday, August 13th, 1903: After a good night's rest we were up and dressed and packed our grips and had breakfast at 6:30. We then started for Yellowstone Lake 20 miles away. It was a charming drive along the Firehole River in the early morning but rather cool. My heavy coat was so comfy. We soon came to Keppler Falls, quite a beautiful scene. The water tumbles over a series of shelf-like rocky benches, making many little cascades over a space of, perhaps, 150 feet. In the bright sunshine of the slanting rays of the morning sun as the water went dashing and frothing down the declivity, it seemed as if covered with a veil of lace. All around was the primeval forest of pines and firs. The singing birds and the gorgeous wild flowers served to enliven and beautify the lovely scene.

Then we left the Firehole River and drove up Spring Creek Canyon a wild rocky gorge shutting out all thought of a civilized world. Arriving at the Cold Spring we halted to drink delicious, refreshing water, such as reminded me of our spring water at home. We toiled up, up, until we reached the Continental Divide, 8,350 feet above sea level. Here the waters flow into the Pacific on one side and into the Atlantic on the other. Then we drove down, down, and then up again until we again crossed the Divide for the last time. After driving through Craig's Pass we again reached an eminence from where we had a fine view of Shoshone Lake and the tall peaks of the Tetons, 14,000 feet above sea level. The eminence is called Shoshone Point and the view is magnificent and grand beyond description. A sudden turn in the road brought us to Lake View from where we have a wonderful view of Yellowstone Lake shimmering in the bright sunshine. This lake is high up in the mountains and is the largest body of fresh water in America at such an altitude. Its water is quite cold and very clear, almost transparent.

From here we descended by easy stages and at last arrived at the Lunch Station on the lake. We alighted and made our toilets for lunch, as we were quite dusty. We were also quite hungry and with our mountain appetite everything was eaten with relish. The great bunches of wild flowers which adorned the tables made us eager to gather some. After luncheon we started out in quest of wild flowers. We were gone so long that Doctor came to seek us and was quite vexed, saying "the boats will not wait all day for you!" How he made poor little Mrs. Livingston and me hustle. A boy had come over from the boat landing to pilot us. The coaches were to go to the lake camp by road while we were to cross the lake to the same place in the little steamboat.

It was well we had a guide to show the way to the steamboat dock though doubtless Doctor also knew the way. It was through a strange and uncanny region of hot water pools and steaming paint pots and hissing geysers. The entire formation was covered with hot water so that one had to pick one's way very carefully over the surface. A new geyser and a new paint pot had burst out here during the summer. I regretted that we delayed our coming across this region and now had to hurry so. I would like to have had time to view it more leisurely. It was a weird and wonderful place. Hurrying along the shore of the lake we stopped a moment to see the famous Fishing Cone a few feet from the bank. Here one may catch a trout in the lake standing on the cone and by lowering the fish still on the hook into the boiling water in the cone it is soon cooked. This may be done also at several places on the Firehole River in the Upper Geyser Basin. There is a lunch station of the Transportation Company here in a plain wooden building.

The shrill whistle of the little steamer called us aboard. She is a steel boat with her name "Zillah" on a white flag floating at her masthead. We were soon steaming out into the lake. The Captain's name was Waters, a good name for a steamboat captain. We found quite a number of tourists aboard who had entered the park by way of Monida and up the Madison River Valley. Our boat fare was included in the Wylie charges but each of the others had to give up $3.00 for the lake trip. That is where the "kick" came in. Mrs. Livingston and Mrs. Littlefield were sitting among(?) them and were much amused at their complaints. Miss Lillian Ehlert was soon at the wheel steering under the care of the pilot. Doctor Henshall and Dr. Donaldson and I sat in the bow of the boat. The scene was very beautiful and as I had not been on the water since leaving Florida it was all very fascinating to me. Upon the mountains was a vague blue efflorescent haze like the bloom upon a grape that made the tint deeper, richer, softer, whether it were the deep blue of the farthest reach of vision of the somber gray of the nearer mountains or the densely verdant slopes of the foot hills that dipped down into the dark shadowy waters of the lake.

The day was somewhat cloudy. Along the western shore was the Absaroka range of mountains and in one place was seen the profile of a human

153

face formed by two peaks of the lofty range. The face is upturned toward the sky and is known as the Giant's Face. It was several minutes before I recognized the resemblance and then I wondered at my stupidity. Mrs. Littlefield said that her daughter had made some sketches of this locality and among them the Giant's Face. We stopped at Dot Island, a tiny green isle in the middle of the lake on which are a number of animals: buffalo, elk, deer, and antelope. They were fed with hay from the steamboat while we were there. Miss Lillian Ehlert, the "awful girl" climbed on top of the corral. The Captain warned us not to go near as the big bull buffalo was very fierce and dangerous and was likely to butt down the fence. He finally did make a terrific rush and butted the fence until I feared the structure would go down before his fierce onslaughts. He was the last animal fed and Doctor said that was the cause of his demonstration and it was all for effect and to get us to go aboard again as the Captain wanted to get the passengers to land at his curio store in season. The men brought another bale of hay and fed the big buffalo that suddenly became very docile.

I guess the Doctor was right as we left the buffalo quietly munching his hay. Soon we were again steaming over the lake. We three again took our place in the bow and thought it queer that others did not seem to want them. We were told that the "Zillah" was brought from Lake Minnetonka, Minnesota, in sections and put together at the lake, which seemed wonderful to me as she has a steel hull. Too soon our journey was at an end. During the afternoon we could see rainstorms amid the mountains and just as we landed at the wharf near the Lake Hotel a gentle shower greeted us. Walking along the pier we climbed the incline to the bank. We passed Captain Waters house and garden and stopped at his store to look at and buy curios and souvenirs. A young giant, either a hunter or a miner, was buying stores. Miss Brush, the tallest lady of our party scarcely reached his shoulder. I watched him as he loaded his purchases on his packhorse until the burden loomed high on its back. Mounting his saddle horse he rode away. The hotel here is quite a large one and they were building an addition larger than the original building with the intention of making it a summer resort during the season.

From the store we walked to our camp for the night. The walk over a dirt road seemed rather a long one to me, but fortunately there had not been rain enough to make it muddy though it proved somewhat dusty under the trees. The camp was very picturesque, situated in a grove of pines with a fine view of the lake. Here we were provided with comfortable tents and plenty of warm water. As we had arrived so late it was necessary to dine without making much change in our attire and could not even comb our windblown hair to our satisfaction. The dinner was good as were our appetites. The water of the camp is supplied by a cold mountain brook. After dining most of our party returned to the store to supplement their purchases. However, Mrs. Livingston and I took a walk through the woods in search of wild flowers and afterward wandered to the shore of the lake as the twilight lingers so long. Near the road is a monument of the U.S. Geological Survey, a block of stone nearly three feet high containing the follow data: 1892, Altitude 7741, Latitude 44 degrees 33.1' 16", Longitude 110 degrees 23' 43.1" W. Magnetic deviation 19 degrees E. When we returned the campfire was blazing brightly though the others had not returned from the dump ground of the hotel where they had gone to see the bears.

Friday, August 14, 1903; After breakfast we resume our journey to the Grand Canyon of the Yellowstone. Our way lay mostly along the Yellowstone River. The first object to interest, except the river, was the Mud Geyser of Mud Volcano. It was on a hill near the roadway, a great pit perhaps thirty feet deep, so filled with steam that we could obtain only occasional glimpses of it. The mud was of a purplish-blue-grayish hue. The trees around the pit were dead and coated with the peculiarly colored mud that had been thrown out. There was something uncanny, fascinating, and weirdly awful about the place. Every now and then the confined steam would gather sufficient force to throw out great chunks of mud that settled back again in the crater. The mud was boiling hot and the roar and rushing of steam was so great that it was with difficulty that one could hear one's neighbor speaking. The explosive bursts were truly terrific. We were compelled to leave the place at last. To me it was the most awful of the many awe-inspiring sights of the park.

We journeyed to Sulphur Mountain. The dust was almost suffocating and the smell of sulphur was "heard in the air." The mountain was as white as lime and resembled it with streaks of yellow from sulphur to orange. At its base is a sulphur pool always boiling and the water that flows from it leaving a yellow coating on the rim. The scene, as a whole, seemed like one of my fantasy dreams. While crossing Alum Creek, beyond Sulphur Mountain, the driver told a story current in the park of how Captain Chittenden, the engineer in charge of the park, once crossed the creek in early days with a big wagon and a four-horse team, but when he reached the opposite shore he was driving a baby carriage and four Shetland ponies owing to the extraordinary astringent properties of the alum in the creek! We next crossed the Hayden Valley, a broad, verdant, grassy park along the river extending for miles. It was formerly a fine range in winter for elk and buffalo.

When we stopped to water the horses at a convenient place on the river we saw trout swimming in great schools, the water being crystalline in its clearness. Once we saw a mink swimming just below the surface of the stream, its tail spread out behind like a trailing feather. Numerous white pelicans were flying up and down the river; occasionally one would plunge into the water with the velocity of a cannon ball. It was a surprise to me that the violent contact of bird and water did not result seriously, as it dived from so great a height and with such swiftness. The trout leaping from the water gave the reason for the plunge I suppose and the concussion was probably to stun or confuse the fish when it would be instantly swallowed. There were flocks of ducks and many bitterns. Our driver told us of a tree not far away on which a white man had carved his initials in 1819. We next passed the bridge being built from the bank to an island above the Upper Falls of the Yellowstone and then, Oh then, we saw the verge of the falls, a mighty volume of water with foaming crest, rushing, and tumbling, with a thundering sound as it pitched over the sheer precipice. Then we got a view of it from the road below, a falling mass of feathery water.

Turning a sudden curve in the road we reached our camp for the night. It was beautifully situated on a woody bluff. Lunch was waiting for us, which we were soon discussing. After luncheon we again embarked on a trip to the Grand Canyon. How can I describe the matchless wonder and beauty of it all. Much has been written; much has been pictured of its marvelous beauty. I sat breathless; I could not speak. I did not want to talk and did not want anyone to speak to me as the tears ran unheeded down my cheeks. The cliffs showed all colors glowing in the afternoon sun. All the shades of red from dark to the faintest pink; all the browns from Van Dyke to ochre; from deepest yellow to creamy white; all the greens from terre verte to the brightest cinnabar are mingled and shaded deftly into one another until one cannot tell where one ends and another begins. Then there is the immensity of it. Castellated rock and cathedral-like spires of jagged crags loomed up far below. Looking down, down, down to the seemingly narrow ribbon of the Yellowstone River as it dashed from steely-blue and silvery-white to pools of emerald green racing around rocks and over stony riffles one knew it was seventy feet wide but could not realize it for the distance down is 1,200 feet. When I got back to the surrey I buried my face in my hands with my head on my knees. Our driver said, "Do not feel so embarrassed, Mrs. Henshall, nearly all my ladies cry." I replied, "I'm not embarrassed," "I feel as though I could die could I be assured that in the life to come I could wander to and fro, up and down, this wondrous canyon forever." Incoherent? Rather. I felt incoherent. Talk of eyes that see not when God hath made such wondrous creations that brush cannot paint or pen describe.

I will insert some descriptions written by able writers and try to grasp mentally what they have said, knowing, however, that the half has not been told. We saw a gulch on the opposite side down which one can descend to the river's brink by means of ladders and ropes. The descent is conducted by Tom Richardson, an experienced guide whom Doctor knows well. We saw some people making the descent who looked like ants crawling down the rocky gorge. Once more we resumed our journey, silent, overcome, awed, and overwhelmed. We passed an enormous boulder of granite weighing tons and tons, irregular in shape, dark-bluish gray, the only granite formation for miles and miles. Whence came it? How did it lodge there? As the rock; ask the forest. In the course of time we got back to our camp which was not far from the Grand Canyon. I retired at once to our tent, Number 6, so tired I could not eat or sleep; tired body and soul, yet happy, satisfied, satiated through the sense of seeing. Doctor was ill during the night, the result of climbing in the hot sunshine and the altogether. He was compelled to go out and I advised him to leave the candle burning in order to guide him back again.

Soon after he went out there was the wildest commotion among a pack of coyotes. I knew the sound. I had often heard it before; such wild, shrill, blood curdling shrieking, barking, howling, and yap-yapping. There is no other sound like it. It makes cold chills creep down one's spine even in broad daylight. There is nothing that will cause the hair on a dog's back to rise like the howl of a coyote. I was so worried that I sat up in bed and thought if Doctor did not return soon I would go in search of him. In a few minutes he came, however, chuckling to himself and said that he went into a tent where a candle was burning but made a hasty exit as he heard a strange woman's voice say, "You are in the wrong tent!" followed by much giggling and smothered laughter. I said, "Did you not hear the coyotes?" "Oh, yes. There is a big pack of them out there. They have a couple of bear cubs up a tree and they are crying help, help!" If the mother bear comes there will be such a scattering of coyotes as was never seen before!" He was very unconcerned about the matter and seemed to think it very funny. I did not tell him how frightened I had been or how I had worried about him.

Saturday, August 15th, 1903: No one had heard Doctor go out or return. No one in our tent heard the coyotes wild yelping as they had slept too soundly. At the breakfast table we began to realize that we were almost at the end of this trip. That is, we would today return to Gardiner and Livingston, there to separate and go to our various destinations, perhaps never to meet again. Some were glad the trip was over, though all felt loath to part company for we had been such a pleasant congenial party. Soon we were on our way out of the park. The morning was lovely and the drive charming. We drove through the woods over a high plateau for many miles. We saw miles of newly cut timber piled up as cordwood on each side of the roadway. Our driver said they were widening the road in order that the sun would more easily melt the deep winter's snow which usually did not disappear until July.

We saw several deer cross the road and disappear into the forest on the other side. Afterward we saw a doe standing in the middle of the road looking at us. She remained steadfastly facing us until we could see her beautiful eyes. Then she slowly moved away and was soon lost to view among the pines. Among other things we saw were the Wedded Trees, two tall slender pine trees that were united like Siamese twins about twenty feet from the ground. Soon we came to the Virginia Cascades; a very picturesque falls in a rocky canyon. Then we came to the Devil's Elbow on the old road far beneath us. It was a very sharp curve, quite a dangerous place for two teams to meet. We then continued on to Norris Basin and Willow Camp, our first stopping place where we had lunch. I gathered a few flowers, mostly aconite and bells of Shandon and then we resumed our journey homeward. We had a fine view of the Mammoth Hot Springs again from the road below. Then we passed the big hotel with new arrivals on the veranda and others who were also preparing for the homeward trip.

Soon after passing Fort Yellowstone I saw numerous sandlillies, the white Mentzelia. Our driver gathered some for me, but alas, they were unopened buds and did not open again. Then on to Gardiner where we had dinner. The railway station is a very characteristic and picturesque structure built of logs with the bark on. The windows are formed of many little panes of glass, the frames being set in deep casements. Inside of the ladies waiting room one sees the logs forming the walls, the great rafters and an immense fireplace with a stick chimney piece. There is a curving pavilion at one end with open sides and within this are placed at intervals fir trees in tubs. Before we left Gardner, Doctor bought some views and photos of the park which were just what I wanted. After boarding the train I saw our driver, Mr. Griffith, walking about the station platform seemingly in search for someone. I called out to him "Are you seeking me?" "Yes, I want to say goodbye and tell you how much I enjoyed taking you through the park. If I drive next summer I will try to get some new flowers for you."

Here is a good place to say that I collected eleven plants new to my herbarium of Montana wildflowers and was also enabled to make nine good sketches. Two of the plants were too badly damaged to be utilized. On the train I met some friends who were also returning from a trip through the park although with another outfit. The train was crowded with homebound tourists. Doctor took the precaution of telegraphing for rooms in Livingstone as we had to stay there all night. It was dark when we arrived at our destination and went at once to the Park Hotel. Some of our party stopped at the curio stores to make final purchases of park souvenirs. Mrs. Livingston and Miss Brush were taken in charge by some friends and taken to their home for the night. We were assigned to the writing parlor of the hotel, a large and prettily furnished room with two immense windows and a folding bed. It was all so comfortable and acceptable after living in the "open" for a week. The bellboy, a pretty child of perhaps twelve with great sleepy, blue eyes brought a washbowl and pitchers of water, towels, soap, and a pitcher of ice water. How glad I was to get a refreshing sponge bath after the long day's travel. It was quite late when Doctor came in. He had gone to all the hotels and rooming houses to get a room for Mrs. Livingston and finally located her at the "Albermarle". The hotels were filled to overflowing for the night. I never saw Mrs. Livingstone again as she left for Nebraska at five o'clock in the morning.

Sunday, August 16th, 1904: The next morning we rose, dressed, and went for our breakfast at the new depot. After a week of canned provisions in the park we greatly enjoyed this meal. Doctor had his shoes shined. They really needed it after walking over the white formation of the geysers. During the trip in the parks no one pays any attention to shoes. Some wear rubber overshoes. This is not a bad plan for there is always a good deal of water and hot at that about the geysers and pools. However, I would advise heavy, strong shoes, with thick soles. Also advisable is a short walking skirt that comes to the top of the shoes.

The train was an hour late. We then said "good-bye" to those of our party who were to take other trains and boarded the westbound express for home. We arrived in Bozeman in another hour, where we found our carriage waiting and in another hour we were at home with "Old Glory" waving over us.[7]

---

7 The Henshalls lived at the U.S. Fish Hatchery near Bozeman so the flag routinely flew at their home.

INDEX

Abbott, Miss (Miss A), 67, 68–69, 73

Absaroka mountains, 153–54

Albee, Mr. and Mrs., 139

Alum Creek, 92, 155–56

ammunition supply, 23, 24

Apollinaris Spring, 129, 141

Army, U.S., 111; Nez Perce Indians attacked by, 14, 31n10; park regulations by, 45n7, 83–84, 83n2, 88–89, 116; South Entrance patrolled by, vii. *See also* military escort

Army Corps of Engineers, vii, 100–101, 115, *120*

Arnold, A.J., 17, 23

Arthur, Chester A., 65

Bassett, Messrs., 77

Bath Lake, 103–4

bear, 12, 83–84, 95n3, 128, 158; cinnamon, 80, 94–95; garbage eating, 142–43, 142n3; stories about, 115–16, 126, 126n3; Synge party approaching, 98–99

Bear Canyon, 138

beaver, 125, 145

Beaver Canyon, 75

Beaver Lake, 101, 144

Becker, E.T., 114

Beehive Geyser, 91–92, 148–49; Synge, G., soaped by, 74, *76*, 90–92

Beesley (guide), 78, 86

Beryl Springs, 146

Bessie, Sarah Jane. *See* Tracy, Sarah

Big Hole Battle, 16, 22, 22n5, 27

Big Hole River, 14

birds, 81, 101, 144

Biscuit Basin, 151

Black, Leander, 2n1

Black Growler, 130, 144

Black Sand Basin, 151

Blaine (horse), 86, 92

blazed trail, 5, 5n4

boating, 18, 112; of Tracy, S., vii, 5, 5n3, *8*; on Yellowstone Lake, vii, 5, 5n3, *8*, 11, *143*, 152–54; on Zillah steamboat, *143*, 153–54

Boiling River, 103, 104, 104n8

Bolly (horse), 85–86; Synge, G., riding, 77, 78–79, 83

Bottler, Phil, 2

Bottler Ranch, 10, 31, 33; military escort to, 7, 9

Bozeman, Montana, 30–32, 33; Federal Fish Hatchery of, 137, 160, 160n7; to Gardiner, 137–39; to Mammoth Springs, 1–3

Brush, Miss, 139, 154, 159

161

About the Author

M. Mark Miller is a fifth generation Montanan who grew up on a cattle ranch in southwest Montana about ninety miles from Yellowstone Park. His interest in early park travel began when he was a little boy listening to his grandmother's tales of cooking bread in hot springs and throwing red flannel underwear into geysers to tint the next eruption pink.

He worked for Montana newspapers while in college at the University of Montana. After graduating, he was a reporter and editor for newspapers in Utah and Kentucky. He earned a doctorate and became a journalism professor at the Universities of Wisconsin and Tennessee.

Miller returned home to Montana in 2003. He has been researching Yellowstone Park history since then and has a collection of more than four hundred first-person accounts of early travel to Yellowstone Park. Two Dot has published his narrative history about tourists who tangled with the Nez Perce, *Encounters in Yellowstone: The Nez Perce Summer* of 1877, and two of his anthologies of such accounts: *Adventures in Yellowstone: Early Travelers Tell the Tales* and *The Stories of Yellowstone: Adventure Tales from the World's First National Park*. In addition, he has published a mid-grades novel about a fourteen-year-old boy's adventures in Yellowstone Park in 1871.

Miller's articles on Yellowstone Park and Montana history have appeared in *Montana Quarterly*, *Big Sky Journal*, and the *Gallatin History Quarterly* (formerly the *Pioneer Museum Quarterly*). He also lectures on park history to various civic groups.

He lives in Bozeman where he has been a volunteer at the Gallatin History Museum since 2004.